The Minions of Chaos

By Dante B. Kun

The Minions of Chaos.

By Dante B. Kun Copyright© 2017. All rights reserved, including the right to reproduce this book or portions thereof in any form whatsoever

A workbook for transition and change.

ISBN: 978-0-692-16354-2

Dedicated to the quest for true freedom within all people everywhere.

I am a being becoming

I allow myself the freedom to become who I truly am

For I am a child of an unlimited cosmos

A co-creator

And that is enough

Dante. B. Kun

Foreword

I am going to give you some rules first. Usually this is something for later on in the book. You might not be crazy about them right now. You may believe they are impossible or unattainable. They are not insane, impossible, unattainable, or unrealistic. They are awesome because they are entirely possible. They are beautiful because they involve your relational self-interest. By the end of this book I am confident that you will love these rules. I will remind you later to read them again. I hope this becomes a habit.

The rules of relational self-interest.

It is not in your relational self-interest to stay in any relationship that is ruled by habitual deceit, dishonesty, cruelty, dysfunction, and violence.

You can leave any situation where you feel unloved. This includes leaving toxic family members as well as romantic partners or negative "acquaintances." People incapable of empathy or compassion cannot "love" anyone. They cannot be authentic "friends "with anyone. You cannot "fix" them. Staying around abusive idiots because they are "family" has destroyed countless lives. Don't fall for the myth of "They are family." You had no choice in the family you were born into. You do have the choice to reject mistreatment, abuse, and insulting behavior.

You can choose to be "Better off without them." This is a perfectly rational decision.

You can leave any relationship that is destroying your capacity for growth, self-acceptance, and self-love. This also includes leaving or avoiding harmful relatives, love interests, work place idiots, and "friends." Insults and negative judgements both obvious and veiled, are completely unacceptable.

You can reject shaming language directed at you by anyone. You owe no one an explanation as to why you choose to avoid them. Shaming language is just cruelty in a weak disguise. Shaming language is sadistic language. Shaming language is always an attempt to control you.

You can decide to go "No contact" with anyone who is abusive, disrespectful, rude, insulting, crass, vulgar, or derogatory towards you. You do not have to explain your decision to anyone.

You can leave anyone at any time who tries to keep you enmeshed within the darkness of pain, guilt, regret, and insult. The past cannot be changed. Actions and beliefs in the present moment direct your future. You are under no obligation to allow abusive people to influence your present moment. No one has the right to constantly use your past against you. Using your past as a weapon to hurt, control, or shame you is automatic grounds for rejection. Relational violence does not have to be physical violence to cause lasting damage.

You do not have to stay trapped in any location, city, or town. Don't sacrifice your inspiration, happiness, or personal aesthetic for a dismal location. It may take work and careful planning, but you can leave.

You, and only you are the final authority on what is important to you.

You are allowed to "begin again." This means unlimited fresh starts and do-overs. No exceptions to this rule.

You define your life path, no one else does this for you. Don't allow them to even attempt it.

Life will offer its ongoing lessons and they will continue in many new forms as well as old forms until you learn from them.

You and only you decide your personal reality, including gender, attraction, beliefs, spirituality, and what makes you happy. Attraction is not a "choice." Your personal aesthetic is authentic because it is something intrinsic to you. Attraction, gender, beliefs, and spirituality are uniquely individual traits. No one else's opinion matters regarding your personal choices. They belong to you alone.

You are allowed to leave when you are hurt emotionally, physically, or psychologically. You need only your permission to do so.

You and only you decide what hurts you emotionally, physically, or psychologically.

You can put your healing first, at anytime and anywhere.

You can reject anyone who wants to keep you enmeshed within an abusive dynamic. (This especially includes harmful, dangerous, cruel, and abusive family members.)

You can allow kind, understanding, and authentic people into your life.

You can allow healthy love into your life.

You and only you select your support team.

You can forgive yourself for all current and past errors involving judgement, misdeeds, imperfections, or wrongdoings.

You can release the past whenever you decide to do so.

You can change directions at any time you choose to do so. Making the decision to no longer stay trapped with toxic people in negative spaces is not "Being weak," "giving up," or "quitting." It is having the strength to seek a healthier way of being in the world. It is seeking to empower yourself and love yourself. It is honoring the drive and need to create a new life for yourself. It is being honest with yourself when you finally realize an old way of life has become invalidated by new growth.

You are allowed to decide for yourself when to move on and when to stay hopeful. You are the best person suited for that decision.

You can admit that leaving the abuser is part of your relational self-care.

You can ignore other people's negative expectations, negative messages, labels, and shaming language, as well as your own negative self-talk.

A little insight about this book:

This is a book that focuses on relationships between people. It can help you take back your life from an abusive predator. Abuse has a dysfunctional signature that can be recognized by healthy people. This signature is an inclusive one. It spans relationships both traditional and "non-traditional." It spans cultures, sexes, genders, identities, and sometimes it defies rigid classifications. My overall goal is concerned with helping you survive emotionally, psychologically, and possibly even physically both during and after a nightmare relationship. The main focus however, is to help you learn how to thrive after freeing yourself from the vampire that is (or was) using you as a source of energy, resources, and supply. It is not my goal to diagnose anyone, nor should you attempt to diagnose anyone. My intention is to help people who are trapped within toxic relationships gain their autonomy and freedom. My desire is to promote awareness and healing for people who have suffered the predations of the psychic vampire commonly known as the narcissist. I am not happy with that particular label but more on that later. The content has been shaped by my day to day interaction with inmates, parolees, and probationers from the California State Prison system, the Alaska State Prison system, county jails, substance abuse treatment centers, and the Federal Prison system. For two decades I have worked with thousands of inmates, addicts, and parole violators. Some preparing to exit the system, and some already out of the system. I taught anger management and conflict resolution at Pelican Bay State Prison for fifteen years. I have encountered narcissists, severe sociopaths, and victims of narcissistic abuse within prison walls. Many of my clients who are struggling with substance abuse challenges are themselves victims of narcissists and sociopaths. My sole focus is to find tough answers and survival strategies for the victims of narcissists, (and cluster B types in general.) I have noticed that these victims are the people usually ignored and seldom focused upon. Victims of a system that often excuses the narcissist and even helps the narcissist cause further harm. The current system only creates suffering, both to society and to the people who are unfortunate enough to become a source of supply for "The Minion of Chaos," The Narco-path. While this is definitely a book of "Relationship red flags," it is much more than that. This is a solution-based book and escape manual all in one. I will use the term "Narco-path," "narcissist," "Creature," and "vampire" interchangeably throughout this book. I do this because, like the fictional vampire, these abusers will drain you of your life force if you allow them to do so. I want to be clear on one important point however. This is not a book to use to "diagnose" anyone. For me "narco-paths" are just part of a spectrum disorder that includes the "Cluster B's" in general and sociopaths in particular. For more on Cluster B disorders I recommend you go to your search engine and type in "DSM-5 cluster B disorders" and strap in for a fun ride. Just for even more fun Type in DSM-5 and sociopath. These disorders are considered untreatable by many clinicians. Challenges to the sociopaths and cluster B folks share some common ground involving impulse control and emotional regulation. These are "nice terms" that really do not address the true destruction wrought by these creatures. These sanitized terms do not do not address the challenges to victims of these monsters. More on that later. A battle wages on between "experts" regarding treatment success with cluster B folks and sociopaths. To date neither side has won. Both sides claim "victory." There are losers however. The victims of the "cluster B chaos spectrum" (my term) are largely ignored and unheard by the "experts." The people involved with abusive, dysfunctional, and dangerous people continue to suffer. This book is for people who have survived their own personal sociopath, narcissist, borderline, histrionic, or anti-social "vampire." This book is for those who seek freedom.

Some signs of relational dysfunction are:

You feel "Love" and loyalty to an abusive, controlling, idiot. You want to keep the relationship going despite constant lying, violations of trust, and ongoing psychological and/or physical abuse. Your love life resembles a dark circus act rather than a loving relationship. You know healthy change should be on the agenda, but you avoid reality. The hurtful, abusive, and dysfunctional interactions outnumber the loving interactions and you cannot seem to change the dynamic. When deep down you desperately want the relationship to finally end but you cannot seem to make it happen, you are in deep trouble. You may be trauma bonded. If you feel "addicted" to your vampire and hope compulsively that things will change, you are trapped, temporarily at least. When the toxic chaos of your "normal" daily life has become your accepted relationship with a dysfunctional vampire, you are in "trauma drama."

The vampire's toxic dynamic may seem normal and familiar to you due to a childhood filled with chaos, mental abuse, verbal abuse, or physical abuse. You may need an understanding therapist to help you untangle the webs that trap you currently. (If you are lucky enough to find one.) You may also need some time with only yourself just to learn how to breathe again. Your relational self-interest must be examined on a healthy continuum. If you feel that your relationship is ruled by the moods and manipulations of your chosen Vampire, then you have given away your own personal power. If you feel any kind of a "Bond" with the energy draining leech that has become your "partner" then it is time to change this toxic dynamic. You will know that this is the case when you accept being treated cruelly as "normal." When you think of your "True love" and you feel fear, confusion, and sadness, it is time to think about your life. Think deeply. The bond between a domestic violence abuser and victim is a classic example of trauma bonding. Another example of trauma bonding occurs between addicts and codependents.

Trauma bonded: This often happens due to a childhood whereby a child was abused intermittently. It is characterized by episodes of "kindness" interspersed with unkindness. For example: a child who is beaten by his mother, yet she buys him toys to "make up" for the beatings. Sometimes she might hold him tenderly and "explain" herself after hurting him. The abuse does not have to be physical. Adults can become trauma bonded. Relational abuse such as insults, shaming language, neglect, aggressive posturing, infidelity, gaslighting, and mental cruelty, coupled with fake kindness and "love bombing" can also cause the reinforcement for trauma bonding. This kind of harming/kindness reinforcement is difficult to overcome. It can become the "Normal" for an abuse victim and she/he can find themselves in abusive relationships that seem to be cyclic. I believe it was Patrick Carnes that developed the term "Trauma Bonding." Chaos, mental or physical pain, and not feeling safe coupled with false "Love" and toxic manipulations are a recipe for a lifetime of abusive relationships if not addressed.

One of the most powerful traps used by Narcopaths and abusive people in general is the illusion they offer with empty promises. These toxic fantasies fuel your hope for better days. Your present moment relationship is based on an illusion. You have bought into a relational dynamic that does not actually exist. The false promises have been made but they are never kept. You find yourself hoping for the false, "happy ever after" to finally manifest. This is a sure and predictable impossibility. You can hope and desire for positive outcomes, however this is just pleasant fiction. The emptiness within the false future promise is only a toxic void into which you pour energy and life force. The lies of the abuser have no chance to finally become real. The vampire assures you that the violence will stop and "I will never hit you again." He/she promises sincerely to "Never again" surf porn sites or hook up sites however the vampire never follows through. The abuser promises to never cheat again, but you find out different. If you are always hoping for a better future outcome while feeling trapped within current misery, you are "future tripping." You are living in a hoped-for future that has not happened yet. Worse, this false future can never happen with your chosen vampire. Always hoping (and working) for him/her to change for the better just causes you to lose focus on what is happening currently. You are losing your present moment reality. You are losing your precious and finite life, moment by toxic moment. You cannot change anyone. Hoping for "better days" will only keep the toxic dynamic flowing. You are cooperating with your captor. Your life is being drained by the vampire minute by precious minute.

Abusers manipulate in many devious ways. False promises are a huge red flag that is worthy of your examination. You must learn to act in your own relational self-interest. This is a skill you can master. Vampires will give themselves away by their false promises. This is one of their toxic patterns. The vampire will swear that he will never yell, hit, push, steal, gamble, drink, (Place lie here) however he never follows through. When you choose to believe a promise made by an abusive person, you are helping them to create an illusion of what you want in a partner.

You are in love with an illusion, you are driven by false hope. Your compassion and empathy have become tools for the abuser to exploit. You cannot change the vampire. This dynamic is ultimately hopeless. Some decisions we can make. Some are made for us. You cannot "fix" your abuser. Feeling pity for the vampire only helps feed the beast with your energy.

Here are some obvious red flags that indicate you might be trauma bonded:

Constant, ongoing dishonesty within the relationship that you accept without thinking about it. Constant fights over the same toxic behavior. There is never any real attempt to address the conflict. You know deep down that your partner is not attempting to communicate authentically. You sense that communication is really a competition that the abuser wants to win at all costs. (Costs to you.)

Abusive language, shaming language, and demeaning insults have somehow become the "normal" language of communication used by the narcopath. You have become acclimated to the exaggerated eye rolls and rude posturing. You have been admonished to "man up," or "put on your big girl panties." You have become used to hearing words like "cunt," "whore," "bitch," "dickhead," "pussy," "coward," "freak," etc. This has become your new "normal."

Ongoing toxic conflicts that are never resolved. You feel forced, manipulated, or coerced into accepting a relationship dynamic that frightens, shames, or upsets you.

(Like constantly failing to keep promises, or continuous insults and put downs thinly disguised as "humor.")

You find yourself trying to change yourself to fit the Narcopaths toxic lifestyle/relationship demands. Your efforts at change only leave you feeling further enmeshed within the abusive relationship.

You find yourself trying to "change" the vampire by hoping to reason with an unreasonable, selfish, dysfunctional creature devoid of compassion or empathy. Every attempt at healthy resolution or constructive feedback is made with (your) idea of "Fixing things."

Your friends tried to warn you initially about red flags they perceived. The friends you currently have left in your life are constantly encouraging you to leave the idiot. Acquaintances, friends, and (Healthy) family members are amazed that you stay in the relationship.

Old sayings like "can't live with them, can't live without them," "boys will be boys," or "happy wife, happy life" have become toxic affirmations that rule your mind. If you feel entrapped yet also accept the entrapment and resist healthy interaction or healthy separation, you need help.

You always seem to be involved in a gunfight armed with only a pocket knife. Your Vampire always goes for the jugular vein or aims for the heart and head. Conflict is a toxic contest with the abuser always winning by wrecking you emotionally, psychologically, or possibly even physically. Disagreements are always characterized by insults, profanity, unfair tactics, cruelty, and degradation. You are always in a psychologically lethal contest, not a normal discussion or disagreement between healthy partners. Mutual understanding is never the goal with an abuser. Power and control are the goals.

Deep down you dislike the vampire, but you are still finding that you do not want to separate. You do not trust the abuser, but you still stay and endure abuse anyway.

You find yourself unable to stop obsessing over the vampire, worrying about their conduct on line or in public. You are afraid of what you will find when you get home. (Or what will happen when they come home.) This has become an accepted way of life. You find that Snapchat, twitter, and Facebook scare you. You are afraid to find out what the vampire has posted today. You fear the vampire's e-mails and text messages.

Your make allowances and ongoing excuses for the vampire's toxic behavior. You defend the vampire to others who point out his/her predations and cruelty. You force yourself to believe the toxic and made up narrative. You make excuses for the creature's malignant dishonesty. You find yourself covering up for ongoing toxic manipulations and cruelty. You find that excuses for the vampire's toxic behavior have become your new normal. Deep down you know that the abuser's dishonesty hurts you. The lies hurt you regardless of the Narcopaths awareness of his/

her dishonesty. You deserve better. The narcopath is not your creation. You are under no obligation to suffer the vampire's predations.

You feel like you have lost your free will. You feel "stuck" and cannot seem to gather the strength to even attempt any change within the toxic dynamic. You dream of leaving however you cannot muster the energy to do so. Fear, resentment, and anxiety live within your every conscious moment.

The success rate for "healing" Narcopaths is simply non-existent. The victims of these vampires seem hopelessly trapped within a grim and ever circular ritual of deceit, love bombing, rejection, manipulation, emotional, and sometimes even physical violence. Sometimes their vampire suffers consequences and experiences incarceration, probation/parole, re-arrest, re-incarceration and probation/parole yet again. The victims of these vampires are themselves doing life on an installment plan administered by the masters of chaos. All this suffering is expensive to the taxpayers fiscally, and expensive to victims and their families emotionally, psychologically, and sometimes also physically. Many times, the victims of Narcopaths, suffering from narcissistic abuse become incarcerated and enmeshed within a toxic culture of addiction and criminality. Often, they are mis-diagnosed with a cluster B disorder by a clinician who does more harm than good. The Narcissism spectrum is a nasty gift that keeps on giving. It is a modern-day plague.

This almost certain failure to rehabilitate or "heal" a narcopath is ignored within the social service industry as well as the prison industrial complex. The experts only lead us into further chaos. Not one seems to have a definitive answer regarding a viable solution to the harsh reality of narcissistic predatory tactics. (Other than to blame the narcissist's childhood and supposed defects in the Narcissists upbringing.) The victims of these monsters need more than just strong opinions and new versions of the "Blame game." The built-in blame assigned to parents, culture, or environment almost always transforms the narcopath into a "victim." This automatic assumption of the narcopath as a "casualty" makes him (or her) "innocent by proxy." There is a pressing need to look at things differently. The real victims of these monsters need to be given true consideration. Society will ultimately thank us in the long run. I have never been comfortable with the current clinical ideas surrounding NPD. Narcissists for me are obviously on the sociopathic spectrum. I would go further and state that they are on the older psychopathic spectrum. I believe that clinicians who push the idea of NPD as a mood disorder are just being sloppy. To classify NPD solely as a reaction to PTSD is clinical laziness bordering on dishonesty. I completely reject the weak idea that NPD is only a "variant" of depression. I like the term "Narcopath" that is currently making the rounds in online forums that empower survivors and help victims of these vampires recover. Clearly, many Narcopaths are goal driven/instinct driven creatures. I hesitate to call them people however they might be "people" in the sense that other ancient hominids were "Human." This dangerous species will never feel guilt, empathy, nor any remorse for their actions. They will always feel justified in their violations. They are oblivious to the idea of accountability.

My Narcopath abusers could fall asleep like drugged baby's after their insane antics. They could move from one emotional state of being to another like turning on or off a light switch. One could transition from pulling my hair and beating me with a belt buckle to sweetly answering the phone "it's so good you called." Scalding me with hot water while screaming at me and then gently applying Aloe Vera was confusing to my child mind. Another enjoyed abusing my genitals while sexually molesting me. This was her signature move, she was "into" pre-pubescent boys. "Spankings" were brutal beatings. My main narcopath used anything nearby to hit me with, including belts, electrical cords, and coat hangers. Once she used a little league baseball bat. She sometimes bought me toys to "make up" for her insanity. Often, she would loudly praise herself for making a salad. She would announce to all present what a "Great" mother she was due to her salad making skills. Nothing makes sense with a narcopath because nothing is ever communicated without manipulation and mixed messages. The Narcopaths ability to interact without ever co-creating healthy resolution is clearly instinct driven in many cases. I believe this as sure as the ocean has currents. I believe that one day science will prove that many Narcopaths are simply following the instructions of their DNA. They are just naturally exhibiting the predatory, energy leeching, manipulative skills and instincts they were born with. These instincts are not learned behaviors, they reinforce and direct the Narcopaths devious skillset. They are intrinsic tools, inborn to the sub-species that possesses them. Narco-paths have no conscience. They lack empathy. They are strangers to compassion. They are built that way. I think there are clearly exceptions, but these exceptions are not the rule.

This situation is one sided but not hopeless. Within this workbook you will find some important personal questions. These questions will address life itself and one's personal relationship to life. They are especially focused upon who we choose to share our precious moments of life with. This book will examine how one approaches life, what judgments about life we hold, what expectations we hold, as well as the finite reality of life. The reader will be challenged to examine how well these thought constructs serve the higher good of society as well as one's self. Your ability to understand healthy "relational self-interest" will be examined and possibly challenged. Some of your core beliefs might also be challenged.

Current treatment programs for the vampires (and the victims of these vampires) are simply not working very well. At tens of thousands of dollars per inmate, addict, domestic violence perpetrator, domestic violence victim, and probationer/parolee, per year, society must go in new directions regarding programs. Narcopaths simply cannot be transformed into healthy people. Taxpayers, (who are forced into supporting this insanity by their governments) are doomed to become financial victims themselves. Forced into supporting these giant holes into which society pours money. As a society we cannot keep on continuing and perpetrating the old ways of doing things and not make the taxpayers suffer. Maintaining the status quo only ensures the victims of narcissistic abuse will continue to suffer. The humble suggestions within the following pages constitute a strategy for victims to find healing. A strategy that is not only about personal survival, freedom, and positive outcomes, but about the social world we all must ultimately survive and hopefully thrive within. This is a manifesto for survivors. This is a way to take back the power we have given away. If an answer exists, it exists within the hard-won insights of survivors. The actions taken by the survivors of these monsters can become a roadmap for success. The social service "experts" have only created and sustained a deeply divided system ruled by chaos. They have enabled the "Minions of chaos" to survive and thrive. The parasitic creature (Narcopath) is allowed and even encouraged by therapists to mimic emotions it cannot possibly feel. The same old boring method is always followed when a therapist is facing a narcissist. A superficial "Assessment" is completed. After the assessment the narcopath is labeled, (Identified as a victim) and blame is assigned, (almost always to parents, siblings, or family members.) Narcissism is routinely blamed on something that happened in childhood. The

Narcopath is "treated," with "counseling." Sometimes these vampires are actually sent to treatment groups with vulnerable people. Within the safety of a process group they gain new manipulation skills and groom new victims. They routinely do this right in front of the oblivious group facilitator. The treatment process varies widely depending on the therapist involved. There is no standard of care that applies. Therapists are often allowed to "wing it" with little oversight. The creature is expected to somehow grow compassion and empathy during the process. Usually the victims go through the entire process ignored, unseen, marginalized, and wounded. Many times, there is no viable assessment completed on anyone involved. Only the highly questionable word of the narcopath is all that is considered. Drama and toxic narcissistic/sociopathic/cluster B manipulation generally rule the process.

How to use this book

At the end of each chapter there will be affirmations for you to use, modify, or change in any way that fits your personal challenges. This is not a book for narcissists, sociopaths, or other abusive beings. This book is written for survivors. This book is a survivor's manifesto. I will repeat some messages occasionally throughout the book. I will review concepts, patterns, and abusive tactics. I do this because I feel that grasping key concepts is important for your healing. Please note them. Repetition helps retention. This book is not a "standard" self-help book. It is a treatment plan for recovery from narcissistic abuse. I come from the substance abuse model, so I will be addressing some dimensions that help people recover from chemical dependence. I will be helping you recognize the importance of being willing to accept change. I will address accountability. I will help you deal with "relapse" or "continued use" regarding your narcissist/vampire. I will help you learn to create a healthy "recovery environment." Take your time and read these pages with self-love for you are beginning a journey to wholeness. If you were missing a limb people would know that you were injured. When you are in recovery from Narcissistic abuse no one can see your emotional injuries. No one understands that your dopamine reward system has been compromised. Often you are judged for your injuries. Be kind to yourself. Take your time. Other people's opinions do not matter now. Only your opinion matters. In recovery we refer to this as a "healthy selfishness." You are worth your finest efforts. You are learning relational self-interest and self-care.

If you are a narcopath reading this book understand that I did not write this for you. It should be clear that you are a sub-species of human to me. An alternate human that the other humans should be wary of. Something that the modern world should never tolerate. Something that could not survive in the ancient world (unless born into royalty.) A toxic sub-species that feeds on the energy of fellow humans. A demented strain of humanity that only exists to consume and destroy modern humans within the safety of the modern world. I see you as a separate division of primate within our species. One that instinctively and pathologically feeds upon the host species energy, resources, time, and attention. I think you are a mutation on the human family tree. I perceive you as a monstrous, manipulative, treacherous, incurable marauder. A product of sometimes nature alone, sometimes nurture alone, and sometimes both nature and nurture. To me, you are a dangerous, toxic, unnatural predator. You damage relationships, people, systems, and you threaten society. I have witnessed your abusive antics firsthand. While I can manage to summon some empathy for your condition, I have no sympathy for your toxic, destructive, and devious patterns. This is a book for your victims, not for you. Continue reading if you so desire but do so at the risk of being exposed for what you are. Not that it will matter to an inhuman, pestilent, destructive animal like yourself. I know that you can only mimic emotion as you have no true compassion or empathy. Nothing I write will harm your "feelings." Your pathological self-centeredness will protect you. Your feelings can't be "hurt" when you lack feelings. Your emotional mimicry means nothing to me. You might become alarmed at being exposed but that is your challenge, not mine. Just know that the civilized human will always prevail eventually, and to the betterment of all.

This is a book for survivors, not perpetrators. Empathy and compassion do not translate as "doormat." They are strengths, not weaknesses. This is a book written with the intention of helping survivors take back their lives and their power. If you are a survivor reading this, know that I respect your journey, your hard-won lessons, and I wish the best for you.

The Personal Development Questions.

Some chapters will have personal development questions. These questions are here to help you gain social, emotional, spiritual, and interpersonal skills. They are here to help you develop your emotional intelligence and your relational self-care. Ultimately, they are here to challenge you and to help you know yourself better. Your safety comes first so do not write these questions out unless you are in a position where the vampire cannot use them against you. The personal development questions will not have a "Right" or "Wrong" answer. The answers will change as you develop insight and accomplish goals. Some of these questions may be painful for you. *Work through the pain* for sometimes new growth can be a bit uncomfortable. The purpose of each question is to help you recognize the patterns of the vampire in your life. Identifying toxic patterns will help you drive a symbolic stake through its malignant heart and put an end to its nasty predations. The minions of chaos can be recognized, and the universe has put you on notice. You simply cannot continue the old way and not suffer. You cannot continue the old way and not have your family suffer along with you. Your old way of life has been invalidated by a demand for new growth, *and the universe is demanding this new growth immediately. I suggest you listen.*

Learning about yourself and healing your past is one of the greatest things you can do to better yourself, your life, and increase your happiness. Self-healing is a powerful and courageous undertaking. Overcoming your past and growing in new directions can become a catalyst for healing your relationships with your family, society, and most importantly, YOURSELF. An unhappy life filled with chaos and non-stop drama is the predictable outcome of a dysfunctional relationship between yourself and your personally chosen vampire. Every victim believes they "need" their oppressor. They do not need the creature once they cease being victims and become survivors. Insight is a powerful catalyst for healthy change. Growth is not always a comfortable process. True growth takes effort and commitment. Right now, **THIS MINUTE** you can better yourself. Your sincere efforts well spent on your personal growth can help you create a new reality. I wish you great speed and good luck on this new journey to wholeness.

Affirmations.

I recommend that you speak your affirmation within your mind each night as you drift off to sleep. I also think you should repeat your affirmation to yourself for a few moments as you are waking up and preparing for your day. As you go through your day, bring your focus internally to your affirmation from time to time throughout the day. When you experience negative thoughts, overwhelm them with your affirmations. As you go through the chapters use the affirmations daily and feel free to mix them up throughout the week. I recommend that you focus upon only one each day if possible.

If you have become engulfed by the vampire's narcissistic games and negative thinking errors, you have some work to do. You cannot expect to use an affirmation for only a minute or two each day and anticipate a quick result. Every negative and self-limiting utterance and verbal/physical violence behavior you accept from your narcopath is an affirmation all its own. IF YOU CHOOSE TO ACCEPT IT. For your affirmations to be successful you must be willing to use them every day and use them a lot! Affirmations can really help you notice self- limiting thoughts and beliefs because you will use them each time a negative thought comes up. Your awareness of your own internal dialogue will be raised, and you will begin replacing the negative thoughts, insults, assertions, assumptions, and dangerous beliefs of the vampire with positive, life affirming thoughts just for you. This will take some work on your part, but it will become enjoyable work eventually. Remember, your chosen affirmation should be the last thing you say to yourself as you are falling asleep and the first thought on your mind when you wake up each morning.

When you finally realize the poison from the vampire's bite has become infected and is consuming your life, the universe has put you on notice. You simply cannot continue the old way and not suffer. You cannot continue the old way and not have your family suffer along with you.   Your old way of life has been invalidated by a demand for new growth, *and the universe is demanding this new growth immediately. I suggest you listen.*

Contents

Chapter One

Life with the Vampire

"Nobody has the right to define your life for you, except you."

The first thing you must understand is that the Narcopath is a well-practiced, consummate liar. These constant lies are intentional and pathological in one. The narcopath is accomplished at lying because the monster's pathology demands this skill. The vampire has become a master of deception by nature's design or nurture's creation. The creature is so good at deception that it can often enlist (make that manipulate) the help of law enforcement, court systems, Child Protection Services, and social service professionals in his/her quest for control and validation. The vampire will go to extreme lengths with its personal vendetta against its chosen target (YOU) whenever it feels that control is waning. Seeking "couples counseling" with a narcopath is usually an exercise in futility. After all, the popular and often unchallenged narrative for mental health professionals is to see the narcissist as a victim of childhood trauma and not the deranged predator that he is. The narcissist is perceived as a tragic victim with a fragile ego who needs help, understanding, healing, and nurturing for his wounded "Inner Child." Most of the information insisting that narcissists are the victims of childhood abuse or neglect is coming from the mouth of the narcopath itself. One rule of thumb to consider in dealing with a narcopath is to understand that if the vampire's mouth is moving, he/she/it is lying. (I often use the masculine pronoun in describing narcissists because as of now most reported narcissists are men; however, I expect that to change eventually as the female of the species has quite a few narcissists among their numbers.) Sometimes I will refer to the narcopath as "it." I am rather fond of that pronoun. I see narcissists as a relative of Homo-Sapiens. I would have no problem referring to a Neanderthal or other ancient humanoid as an "it."

Let's first understand societal violence. The Narcissist is a master of societal and relational violence. This means that the narcissist will "communicate" with your family, friends, your children, social workers, police, investigators, your employer, people you meet at church, or even possibly people at your gym. The minion of chaos will try to manipulate anyone and everyone who knows you. The vampire will try to exert his evil leverage with your social connections pathologically no matter how important or peripheral they are in your life. The narcissist will want to influence them against you to exert his control. All "communication" attempted by a narcopath is only an attempt to delude someone else. This evil creature will openly and shamelessly lie about you to deceive the people in your life. When you have allowed a narcissist into your world you are in deep trouble. Your vitality and zest for life is in danger. The narcissist is going to do his best to control your existence. The monster will attempt his domination from the beginning of the relationship. The vampire will demand your attention, energy, and possibly your destruction even after the relationship has ended. In the beginning he will use flattery and romance to control you. Eventually he will undermine your self-esteem by subtle (at first) insults to your vision of yourself and how you feel about yourself. For him to accomplish this, you will have to give him the power to do so. Every "Victim" needs their own personal "Oppressor." That means you will have to be willing to accept his opinions as he presents them. In doing so, you are accepting the opinions of a consummate liar, manipulator, and overall creep. Remember, if the narcissists' mouth is engaged, moving, and operating, he/she/it is lying. Narcissists are experts at blending truth with untruth. They will leave out important details and they will include truthful but unimportant details to cloud the issue. Deflection and deception come naturally to Narcopaths. Word salad is something the vampires excel at creating.

The narcissists' only goal is to use you for something. This may be hard for you to believe. The vampire may be using you for money, self-esteem, (his/hers always) status in the community, security, or just for its own sick, twisted amusement. What you "believe" to be true does not matter. This creature does not have the capacity to care about you. This vampire wants something, and it will always be something you have, or some quality you possess. Be it mental, emotional, financial, or physical, the vampire is hungry for your resources. Your energy both positive and negative, is the creatures supply. Once you stand up to the vampire by denying it your resources or energy, it will begin a serious attempt to destroy you. The narcopath loves to destroy its victims within their community. The vampire will laugh at you as it attempts to wreck you financially, professionally, or socially. Campaigns of character assassination against their former supply source are a favorite tactic. Expect twitter, Facebook, snapchat, and social media platforms to become a demented forum for the narcopath to abuse you. This aberrant creature will always seek your destruction once your energy is no longer available. Make no mistake about this fact, Narcopaths are dangerous when you deny them your resources. Societal and relational violence is still violence and it can cost you dearly, especially with the people you love. Smear campaigns are something you can count on when you finally reject the vampire. This is true both pre and post discard.

Remember:

The care and feeding of your narcopath will require great amounts of your energy and time until you make the decision to finally starve the vampire. You will not be able to meet the toxic demands upon your life energy anyway. Don't feel bad about this at all. No one can survive being drained daily. Be it in the form of flattery, money, time, transportation, substance abuse (his/hers,) verbal violence, and possibly even the enduring of physical violence, you will feel that the chaos will never end. The constant drain of feeding the vampires always hungry ego will never stop. Its appetite will consume great amounts of your mental and physical energy. Ongoing chaotic drama is the fuel source that feeds the toxic nature of this beast. He will blame you for the discomfort of his feeding frenzy that ultimately devours your self-esteem along with the relationship. He will then set about to assassinate your reputation and character by using your friends and acquaintances (His personal "Flying Monkeys") to sway to his "side." The toxic vampire will use all of its manipulative and persuasive skills against you to destroy your social, professional, and possibly even physical existence. The vampire will always discard you eventually. It is instinct driven to always seek new sources of energy. Think of "Flying Monkeys" as the Narcopaths fan club. The vampire will always have his fans and sometimes they may include "friends" in common.

These will sometimes include your family members, children, and often even minor acquaintances. "Triangulation" is a manipulation used by Narcopaths to control and manipulate communication. Instead of communicating directly with you, the vampire will involve a third party in the communication chain. The vampire is usually trying to instill jealousy and vulnerability within its chosen food source. "Gas lighting" is when the narcopath tries to make you appear insane and unreasonable. Gas-lighting is also an attempt to make you doubt yourself. Flying monkeys, triangulation, and gaslighting are all narcopath control tactics.

The fact that going "no contact" works with a narcopath just reinforces my belief that narcissists do not respond to therapy. For therapy to become effective there should be authentic interaction of some kind. The predator must somehow come to understand and feel remorse for his predations. The old, destructive way of life must become invalidated by new, healthy growth and understanding. Therapy cannot work to heal a parasitic/narcissistic driven relationship. The vampire is feeding off of his host. You cannot teach an emotionless creature to feel emotion. The non-human, narcopath predator can only mimic emotion in order to survive and feed upon its prey. Going "Grey Rock" and no contact has been shown to work. This would not be so with actual humans who are capable of feeling compassion. Humans are social creatures. Humanity's ability to honor and protect each other via social understanding and interpersonal compromise has been a huge factor in our survival as a species. (Grey rock involves becoming so boring and low energy that the narco-path loses interest in you and moves on to other prey.)

The narcopath almost always has a strong opinion on everything and he wants you to believe that he is competent on every topic. He is often a self-proclaimed "expert" in all fields with no training or actual expertise in any of them. If the narcissist is competent in a field of endeavor, you will never hear the end of it. Count on him to claim expertise in other fields unrelated to his field of expertise. He will still be a legend in his own mind no matter the subject. The narcissist never feels empathy for anyone and all people are there for his exclusive use. When his target has no more energy to drain, be it money, time, or positive/negative attention, the psychic vampire will move on towards another victim. This will be an effortless undertaking for the narcissist/vampire because he/she will "monkey branch" long before actually discarding you. It is easy for this emotionless monster to move from one energy source to another because the vampire invests nothing in the relationship. Monkey branching is a term used to designate someone who starts another relationship right before ending the current relationship. Monkey-branching is exactly like the way a monkey swings from branch to branch and thus goes from tree to tree. The monkey never releases his grip from one branch until he is confident that he has another branch to grasp. This is one of the patterns you can use to recognize a narcissist/narcopath.

How do you recognize that you have a narcopath in your life? You start by recognizing the patterns of the vampire. These patterns are obvious and discernable, and after you learn to recognize them you will wonder at the predictability of the narcissist vampire. Like the mythical vampire, abusers are vulnerable to "light." In order to defeat their nasty predations, you must be willing to shine the "light" of your consciousness and awareness in their dark and murky direction. It is important to remember that listening to what the narcopath is saying is important. It is more important to look closely at what the monster is accomplishing however. Their words will not match their deeds.

Ask yourself some key questions: Are they a constant time bandit? Do they consume your precious resources like money, energy, time, and attention? Narcissists generally love center stage and turn every interaction back to them and their inexhaustible drive to garner other people's energy and attention. They start out by giving attention and flattery, but they always end up using and consuming everything energetically that their host/victim can create or expend. Let's go over some tell-tale signs:

1. You seem to always walk on eggshells around the narcissist because you have been trained to not upset them no matter how mentally cruel

they are to you. You have accepted their twisted terms of existence. You have become a source of supply. You have subconsciously accepted that their needs come first, and you are always a secondary consideration. They can move quickly and seemingly effortlessly from affection to being openly rude, indifferent, arrogant, boastful, and haughty. They have made it clear by their words, deeds, and actions that you are a second-class citizen within their little, twisted empire. Your feelings, thoughts, efforts, desires, and even your existence only has meaning if it serves the vampires twisted scheme. You never know how the minion of chaos will change day to day or even hour to hour. This evil chaos will be your reality once you are enmeshed within the toxic dynamic of the narcissistic/abusive relationship. The fact that the creature pursued you relentlessly in the beginning of the relationship (love bombing) is just evidence of its pathology. The energy they put forth being unstoppable in the "honeymoon" stage means only that they were hungry and needed new supply. All of this is just deception. It means nothing because the vampire is incapable of caring or feeling empathy. The minion of chaos instinctively chose you for your qualities of compassion and kindness. An evil pathology directed him to you. His future predations within your life depend upon you having qualities he can use to manipulate. Narcopaths and empathic people seem to attract each other. You will often find yourself being the "understanding" one in the relationship. You will "understand" because they will have told you all about their many challenges in life. The creature will have "shared" the many cruelties it experienced at the hands of others. Eventually the monster will use this made up past in order to justify the many reasons they have for seeming to ignore you. They will insist they are not at fault. They will also tell you how "crazy" you are (Gaslighting) for not understanding the "obvious." It is always someone else's fault for their behavior, (mostly your fault however.) How dare you not be available at feeding time?

2. Both male and female Narcopaths will often use sex and attention as a weapon to control you. They will shower you with praise and adoration for a brief time in the "Honeymoon" stage of the relationship. Once you are "captured" they will withhold attention and begin to reward your "good" behavior. Only actions they deem worthwhile are "good." These actions on your part may actually be hurtful to you, emotionally, financially, sexually, or professionally. They will shower you with attention, interspersed with put downs. This is just to let you know that you

are "lucky" to even have them in your miserable life. You will be relegated to the position of always being the partner who initiates sex or any kind of physical intimacy. The Narcissist will always make it seem like you are barely deserving of their attention. They love to put out the subliminal message that you are "lucky" that they even respond to your advances. They will act haughty and show by their statements, actions, and facial expressions that they are superior. They can fake emotions well but do not deceive yourself, they are emotionless vampires. They are incapable of empathy or compassion. The only humanity you see deep within the eyes of a Narcopath is your own humanity being reflected back at you. Without reflection, Narcopaths often have dead, lifeless eyes. The eyes of a shark are more lifelike. Their smiles can give them away. Their eyes often do not match their smiles.

3. Your online presence soon becomes modified to embrace their insatiable appetite for attention. Initially they will bombard you with attention online. They will blow up your Twitter feed, Snapchat, and Facebook with messages, pictures, links, "cute" statements, flirting, YouTube videos, and their bullshit proclamations of love. Many female narcissists are famous for the "duck face" selfie. Many male narcissists

like to post pictures with their mouths open as they display surprise or humorous faces. Narcopaths often love to show their tongues for some unknown reason. True narcissists are incapable of any real concern for your feelings and have no capacity to love anyone. They are hoping to condition you to become reliant on their manipulative communication tactics. Their evil pathology is designed to keep you in line and dependent by starving you for attention and rewarding you with attention. This is to ensure that you feed them what they want. They always thirst for your time, money, resources, and energy. They crave your willingness to continue stroking/feeding their giant ego on a constant basis. Beware of the social media stage however because the narcissist only uses online platforms to perfect the image of themselves they want to project to the world. Overt narcissists are easy to spot on social media. They post updates and status constantly. They show lots of pictures with lots of skin visible on an almost constant basis. They think that they must show the world their meals almost every day. They are convinced that the world is fascinated by their every little action. This includes what they put in their mouth, and what comes out of their mouth. They will extol their opinions freely and expect universal acclaim from all who read their posts. Over-expressive selfies and "Dick pics" are their normal photogenic expression. They are positive that they are so important to the world that everyone must want to know their exalted opinion on literally everything on line and off line. If they are not a public figure and they have "friends" that number in the hundreds on Facebook, you are looking at a huge red flag. If they have over a thousand friends and they are not a politician or actress/actor/YouTube personality then run away, run away fast for these people are most likely batshit crazy.

4. In the very beginning of having just met you, they will bring up all the many shared "interests" they have in common with you. Don't fall for this extreme manipulation. It is total projection upon your internal movie screen. The narcopath is projecting (and sometimes reflecting) what it thinks you want in a relationship. The vampire will feed your ego all it can eat, for a while anyway. Then he/she/it will start to feed upon you. The monster will become your own personal energy drain. It will become a toxic time bandit and it will feast upon and consume the precious and finite moments of your life. The narcopath will not care if it takes positive or negative energy from you, just so long as it receives energy from you. The vampire will take all you allow it to take from you. The vampire will do so without

remorse. The vampire will never change, and you cannot "heal" this creature. The vampire will not stop until you stop the creature. You stop the energy leech by starving it.

5. The relationship beginning is almost always super intense. The narcissist counts on an almost chaos level of engagement. Narcissistic/ abusive relationships will generally proceed with unimaginable speed. The vampire will assume a role of familiarity with you that the creature has not actually earned. (Initial love bombing.) The narcissist will literally bombard you with flirtation and romantic communication until you succumb to "Paralysis of analysis." Most normal humans just cannot keep up with the pace and progression of the "relationship." The Narcopath will quickly let you know how "unique" you are in the world. Words like "Special," "Beloved," "One and only," and "Love," may be used as if the relationship has a much longer history than it does. You will quickly be assigned a "pet name." You will feel special in a way you have never experienced. It will seem like a fantasy (because it is a fantasy) and you soon find yourself "Swept away" by the narcissist's attention and praise. "Love Bombing" takes preparation. Narcissists are voracious observers that become voracious communicators when their true colors begin to show. In the beginning, you will be doing almost

all the listening, but that dynamic will change fast. Very soon you will be defending innocent actions and hoping to "not upset" the vampire. You will face false accusations soon enough. The vampire will listen carefully at first and then he will speak constantly until he starts to use the "Silent Treatment" on you. He will find the chinks in your self-esteem for later use. All your secrets will eventually be his to use for blackmail and manipulation. The fiend thinks nothing of lying to gain your trust. Dishonesty is these freaks natural state of being. Your trust will have become a Narcopaths weapon. The vampire will have been delighted by this successful manipulation on its part. It will feed on you constantly. You will be unprepared for this level of instinct driven savagery. You will be feeding an animal in human form. Eventually you will learn that all this was never communication, it was a deadly competition. Your energy was being secured for supply.

6.   The narcissist will use character assassination of others in his/her past by comparing you in a favorable light to certain people in its past. Eventually however you will be compared in an unfavorable light to other people. That is a guarantee. In the honeymoon stage this means you are the literal light of his life and much better than any past lover, past friend,

even past and current family members. You are his "Best friend" and you both have "So much in common." The term "Soulmate" will most likely be used. He may even use terms like "Old soul" or "Transcended." Eventually, when the narcopath cheats on you (and he/she/it will) the vampire will use the same toxic communication and manipulation methods on your guaranteed future replacement. The creature will laugh at you (and ridicule you) as it "Monkey Branches" to another supply source. Remember, the narcissist is incapable of actual love. Real love requires compassion and empathy. These are emotions the vampire does not possess. Monkey branching is a common narcissist tactic. Remember, just like a wild monkey, the narcopath is always looking for a new food source. While hunting, it will not let go of one supporting branch until another is ready to support its weight. The goal of a narcopath is always control. The fiend has an unstoppable desire to feed. The narcissist is a natural and deceptive predator.

7. The narcissist is a master manipulator. The creature is an expert at rationalizing things away at such a lightning pace that a normal human cannot keep up with the non-stop lies and daily deception. One of my friends, Gary N, once described the mental snares of his

female narcopath as a "Steel trap." I thought that was a perfect description of the mental manipulations that narcissists are so adept at creating. The skilled narcissist always has an excuse or "perfectly rational" explanation for anything shady happening currently in the "relationship." They can justify anything shady that has happened in the past. Dishonesty is an art form to the narcopath. They are superficially charming, goal/instinct driven, and socially adept. They use these skills in a deadly fashion. You will experience the creature's "rapier like wit." You will also have to deal with its insanity in the form of irrational arguments that sustain unreasonable behavior. Get used to circular reasoning statements like: "I didn't do it." "It is your fault." "I did it because you made me do it." "If I did do it, it is your fault I did it, so it is the same as if I never did it." Get used to the insanity until you decide to starve your vampire with no contact.

8. You will find yourself off balance emotionally and always feeling that something is not quite right. You will find yourself wanting to check the browser history on their computer or their phone. This is a direct message from your subconscious mind and you should go with this instinct. Something is not right. You have a vampire draining you. Your survival instincts

are not "paranoid." Just because the narcopath has a dull amygdala and a compromised limbic system does not mean you do also.

9. Remember, Facebook, twitter, snapchat, and social media will often become a tool of manipulation for the narcissist. These useful services that normal, healthy humans use to communicate and interact with each other become sinister devices when used by narcissists. They can quickly become a tool of destruction, the destruction of your self-esteem and reputation. Luckily, narcissists mis-using social media are easy to spot. They stand out. Remember, the toxic goal of every narcissist is to use people. The vampire is thirsty for your attention, resources, energy, and time. They want your energy/attention always and this toxic demand gradually consumes your life, but it requires your consent. Minute by minute you allow them to drain your precious life away as long as you stay with them. Jealousy, victimhood, and competition are their romantic lifeblood. These circumstances feed the vampire's insatiable ego. Social media will become the vehicle whereby the narcissist provokes you with petty jealousy via triangulation and rivalry. After all, the vampire can then use one of its favorite weapons, gas lighting. The narcopath will accuse you of one or more of the following: "It is all in

your head," "It is your own insecurity," or their favorite, "You're crazy." All their attention will be directed at this new pastime of creating and sustaining their many and seemingly constant online, drama filled flirtations and competitions. There will be no attention for you anymore. Their previous lovers as well as those they friend zoned will be baited and manipulated with praise, petty intimacy's, and inside jokes that only they share together. You will feel like an outsider. This is intentional. Triangulation will be the goal. This is all done to feed the insatiable ego of the narcissist as they simultaneously destroy your self-esteem and increase your insecurity. The creature will do this well. Your relationship with them will be transformed into chaos. They will feign innocence in a toxic game they created and blame you for being insecure even as they intentionally feed your insecurity. They will always use intimacy as a weapon to control and manipulate you. They will create the toxic relational currency and they will set the unfair exchange rate. They will sell their dysfunction to you at an unfair price, and they will insist that you spend it at the abusive exchange rate they created. The narcissistic relationship is not sustainable. Not for a healthy human anyway.

10. They may use "humor" as a weapon against you. It will begin with veiled insults hidden

in "jokes." They can't help it because the narcissist's toxic nature will eventually reveal itself. They will become condescending when they address you and you will be the brunt of "Back handed compliments." Humorous insults by the narcissist will become part of your normal interactions daily. This is just another tool the vampire uses to undermine your opinion of yourself and destroy your self-esteem. Their pathology directs this dysfunction. It is all executed perfectly so they can control you better. They will insist they mean you no ill will and you are just "Being silly." They will act "cute" and innocent about these constant veiled (and not so veiled) daily insults, threats, and put downs. Once they have succeeded in manipulating you to doubt yourself and they have impacted your self-confidence, they will dig in even harder. You will be spending almost every waking hour dealing with their narcissistic drama and facing their toxic relationship chaos. They will always act as if they are innocent of any manipulation and twist any observations back onto you as a shortcoming on your part." You are too sensitive," or their favorite, the old standby: "You are crazy." They will deny their insulting body language and facial expressions. They will deny their negative voice tone even when it is obvious.

11. You will eventually be doomed to become Sherlock Holmes. You will have no friendly Watson to help you out with the investigation into the madness of your personal vampire. You will find yourself in the strange position of wanting to explore the narcissist's every online picture album, go back into their twitter history and Facebook lineage. You will find yourself snooping on the pages of the narcissist's past love interests, online groups, and close friends but it is all a waste of time on your part. It will only increase your personal chaos and lead to paralysis of analysis. The narcissist is incapable of love and all that history is just a chaos induced lie. It is only a source of energy and attention that is incapable of feeding the predator's ever-hungry ego. That history is only the past manipulation and ego feeding he used on others. The vampires past manipulations, triangulations, gas-lighting, dishonesty, and insanity with others will lead you only into chaos and dysfunction. It is just a vampire's chaotic trail of all that is left of past feeding frenzies. The only things a narcissist can ever add to anyone's life is wreckage and chaos. The narcissist's phone will hold interest for you because the creature will be so secretive with it. (just as he is with his online porn visits.) The vampire is most likely good at deleting the phone's history anyway, so don't bother looking

for it unless a GREAT opportunity comes up. If you do find anything amiss do not expect him to even listen to you when you bring it up. He will simply attack you on every emotional and psychological level available to him. By this time the Narcissist will be accusing you of doing all the nefarious deeds that he is continually engaged in daily. He will be questioning ALL your online activity constantly. He will be checking your browsing history daily and your phone history. He will do this both openly and behind your back. He may even check your mileage on your vehicle after you drive somewhere without him. He will install apps on your phone without your permission. He will install spyware on your computer. You will be accused of his vile deeds daily; it will become your new "normal." It will stay this way for as long as you decide to keep him in your life. It will not improve with time. You will not be able to "fix" the relationship. Things will not get better, things will only become more dismal. You cannot "fix" him. Since the monster is incapable of feeling compassion and empathy, it cannot be reasoned with. There can be no "shared experience." The vampire is immune to epiphanies.

12. You will get used to feeling drained emotionally. You will find yourself spending money you don't have, and money you do have, solely on the

vampire. This will happen on a regular basis. You will become gradually estranged from family members and long-time friends. You will not understand how it all became so dysfunctional. Your life will become a hurricane of destruction, leaving behind a trail of wrecked relationships with friends, family, co-workers, and mentors. It will seem that there is no apparent reason for the death and destruction of all you held dear. However, you will eventually see the truth. The Vampire loves to drain energy and their appetite for your emotional, physical, and financial energy is insatiable. Your life is their supply. If you value and cherish your life, a relationship, or a personal belonging, the narcissist will destroy it in the long run. Your entire life will eventually become consumed by this narcissistic vampire. This is because the narcissist has no end to his/her/its destructive appetites. The monster is toxic, dysfunctional, and in constant need of your attention and energy. It is also instinct driven to desire everyone else's attention and to attempt to control all communication. If confronted with their manipulative behavior the vampire will deny all wrongdoing and flip the script right back upon you. He may use anger bordering on hatred to do this. He may also claim "victim status" to make his poison more palatable. It is imperative that you understand what you are up against. You are facing a vicious, egotistical vampire. His ego is so attached to his position that if his position were to crumble by logic, reason, and evidence, his ego would fall with his position. Thus, the narcopath will go to amazing, ridiculous, and even dangerous lengths to prop up his position. He is instinct driven by his DNA and/or his environment/upbringing. He must preserve his precious ego. This is a contest that you cannot hope to win via logic, reason, or reality. It does not matter in the least if you have truth and proof on your side. This is also the dangerous side to the Narcopath personality that you must consider and become aware of, as it represents a direct threat to your continued well-being. Most toxic narcissists will go on the attack when confronted with logic and reason. Any observation regarding their dysfunctional behavior will be ignored or attacked illogically. Any negative action or statement that they cannot deflect away from themselves will be pathologically resisted by any means necessary. They will try to destroy your relationship with those people who are important to you. They want you isolated from your support network, your family, and your community. They don't want you to have any allies. The vampire desires to control and manipulate from the shadows while occupying center stage in your life.

13. The Narcissist/vampire will always accuse you of their actual conduct, thoughts, and deeds. This is one of their most obvious red flags and it helps you identify them. However you must pay attention to their projections. If you are suspicious of their behavior and suspect them of being unfaithful for example, they will accuse you of being unfaithful. If they are flirtatious online or in public, they will accuse you of being the real flirt. They will accuse you of being "crazy" or "paranoid" for just noticing their behavior. They will accuse you of their actions even as they make a spectacle of themselves on social media in front of anyone who happens to be online. They will blame you for their infidelities. They will bring up the distant past and twist things around concerning your past interactions to make you the offending party. This manipulative behavior will never stop; in fact, it will only increase without direct action on your part. One day you will find yourself wondering how things became so out of control. How love could have become such a twisted mockery of life. How you could be so unhappy, so drained emotionally and so afraid all at once. The narcopath will insist that this situation is all your fault. With a narcissist it is always someone else's fault. They are never culpable for their actions. A narcissist believes that he has no flaws, and they will never

admit any shortcomings or challenges. However, they will gleefully, and pride fully point out all your "faults." They will accuse you of every possible deficiency even as they exhibit daily the "imperfections" you supposedly possess. They will arrogantly point out your "shortcomings" to you. They will also point out all your "failings" to your friends, co-workers, and family. They will secretly complain about you to anyone who will listen. You will become an expert at "walking on eggshells." You will be ruled by fear-based thinking and you will have no clue how it all happened. They will triangulate with deadly accuracy. Your life will be chaos and the chaos will seem "normal."

Do not despair however, as we humans are pattern seeking creatures. The narcopath at his core is an unenlightened animal. He is instinct driven like an animal, not intellect driven like a human. You can and will recognize the narcissist by his conscious and unconscious patterns. Once he is recognized as a hungry predator you will eventually begin to starve this vampire out of your life. You must cut off his supply. If you have children with the monster, you must take control. You can mitigate the creature's deadly habits to spare your children and yourself future emotional, psychological, and physical damage. The vampire's abusive patterns are his greatest weakness: just as sunlight is to a vampire, patterns are to a narcissist. They cannot escape their patterns any more than an animal can escape its instincts. More "light" is the answer not more "heat," because light reveals their patterns. The unflinching illumination of logic and reason reveals their thinking errors, along with their constant logical fallacies. Heat, in the form of interpersonal and relational contention between the narcissist and yourself will only result in causing you more internal conflict. It will only facilitate the generation of useless feelings like guilt, shame, fear, regret, and low self-esteem. Conflict only feeds the narcissist and it loves being fed. Dissension and discord supplies the creature with the personal energy it craves. It is an emotional energy that he can never fully satiate himself with, however he will always seek it. Narcissists are super predators. I know it is not "politically correct" but I still maintain that they are a different and dangerous/defective branch of the human tree that preys upon modern humans. I have no doubt that some narcissists are born and not made. Some are both born and made. The Bible put's it best in that: "By their fruits you shall know them." If you find yourself always under attack socially, emotionally, personally, and psychologically, it is time to pay attention to the toxic dynamic. When you find yourself embroiled in constant drama instigated by your spouse, lover, parent, friend, employer, or co-worker, it is time to take inventory of your life. If you are always doubting yourself, feeling under attack, and feeling hopeless, do not doubt your feelings. You are most likely under narcissistic attack. The "fruit" of the narcissist, what he or she produces in your life, is always drama, chaos, lack, limitation, feelings of inadequacy, fear, desperation, and ultimately, loss. The narcopath always eventually discards what he cannot use any longer. This is a common denominator in all narcissistic relationships. I recommend joining some narcissistic support groups online. If you must create a fake profile so your narcissist/vampire does not know about your activities, do what you must to keep yourself and others safe. When you are stalked online you know you are in trouble and must create some healthy change in your life. Just read the posts from people who are in process of rebuilding their lives after suffering narcissistic abuse from a vampire. Share only if you feel like it. Remember that online you are in control. Use the block button as often as you desire. To deal with any challenge, you must first admit that you face a challenge. It is perfectly OK to learn from others in the same situation. Many times the so called "Experts" simply lead us into more chaos. Narcopaths are proficient in their abilities to manipulate "experts." Many people have lost friends, family, careers, and finances to narcissists who have alienated any outside support their victims may have had in their lives.

The Narcissist's motto is "I did not do that."

The Narcissist's slogan is "It's never my fault, it's your fault I did that." (But I still didn't do it.)

The Narcissist's oath is "I am never at fault. You asked for it, that's why I did it." ("But I still didn't do it and you're crazy for accusing me."

Recognize the game! Refuse to play the game. Narcissists recognize vulnerable people and take advantage of them. Their toxic pathology drives this behavior pattern. Just as the vampire/narcissist wanted your life-blood/energy, you wanted something also. You wanted love, acceptance, companionship, and understanding. The narcissist gave you the initial illusion of your own desires. The vampire reflected your own humanity back at you and you loved what you perceived. You ended up in the wreckage of a failed relationship because you worked at it. You gave the vampire your blood and he drank it. He also surgically removed anyone who might have been able to help you recognize his intrinsic evil. The creature used relational manipulation to force you to accept the demented equation that eventually evolved into the "relationship." You bought into a toxic and limiting relationship that you work so hard to save. He destroyed all your important relationships with family and friends because he needed to ensure his control over you. So, let's recognize the game and stop it from playing out. Once you recognize the game the narcissist plays, it is time to stop playing the game. Move to no contact. If you have children move to limited contact. More on these tactics later. Independence is your goal. This includes being independent of the narcissists opinion of you. Independent of the opinions of his flying monkeys and the people he uses to triangulate. Take back your personal power.

If you can relate to any of this dysfunction then you know something is wrong and you have known for some time. It's time for you to develop a healthy selfishness that will begin to serve your higher good. The narcissist is no "victim" even though the counseling "Industry" views him that way. You have heard the drill by now. The common belief is that the narcissist has low self-esteem due to some reason usually rooted deep in his childhood. Mental and or physical abuse is usually named as the culprit. The only "proof" of abuse needed is the testimony of the narcissist. The narcissist is always perceived as a victim and thus his actual victims are usually ignored or minimalized. Many times the victims of narcissistic abuse are blamed for their condition. This dynamic is very strong in the recovery community. A lot of people in recovery are blamed for their condition, just as people who commit suicide are often blamed for their condition. A lot of time and energy is spent on identifying whether the narcissist is an "Overt" or "Covert" narcissist. I come from the idea of the harm reduction model that we use in substance abuse counseling. I am an advocate for the victims of narcissistic abuse, not the perpetrators. Let's remember and recognize the common theme/propaganda dominating counseling: That the Narcissist uses control and manipulation to make up for his own low self-esteem and his fragile ego. I think this hypothesis is sometimes correct however sometimes it is horribly incorrect. Remember, if the narcissists' mouth is moving, he is lying. Additionally, there is no justification for him to be costing you any of your precious time, resources, and relationships with friends and family. It is all just a tool he uses (Manipulation) to exploit you and those people he needs to influence and control. His goal is to ultimately isolate you from their possible (and often much needed) support. His "victimhood" does not entitle him to destroy even one precious moment of your life. He has no right to manipulate therapists, police officers, your friends, and your family members. In short, anyone who might be able to help you recognize his deadly patterns, for patterns are his one, true, weakness. It does not matter if the narcissist is "Overt" or "Covert" as they both have identifiable personality patterns. Just look for conceit, arrogance, selfishness, hostility, low impulse control, an obvious inability to perceive emotion, and a complete lack of empathy, and compassion. They also demonstrate an overall disregard for the thoughts, ideas, and feelings of other people and bring all interactions back to themselves. They just see other people as tools to an end and not as fellow human beings. The narcissist operates with very specific, identifiable thinking errors regardless if he/she is "Overt" or "Covert."

To bring back wholeness and healing into your life you must learn to identify, recognize, and nullify these thinking errors until you can initiate no contact or controlled contact (If you have children together) with the narcissist. No contact is what will bring you the maximum peace and healing, for you simply cannot heal a narcissist. No one has the power to make that happen. Some things you can change, some things you cannot change, and some things must just be accepted. You can control how you respond to the things you cannot change and the things you can change. Let us go over some common thinking errors the narcissist uses to manipulate his victims regardless if he is "Overt" or "Covert.".

1. Black and white thinking, the false dichotomy, or the false dilemma. This logical fallacy complements the narcissist's competitive way of communication. He is always driving towards "win-lose" outcomes. The narcissist usually presents his manipulative arguments in a way that always places an issue in the form of two extremes of belief. There is no wiggle room or room for negotiation ever. The argument is always an either/or situation. Only two choices

are presented when other choices exist. The narcissist will often present the conflict in a way where you are either for his position or against his position and either way you respond will fortify his position. If you answer in a way he views as positive, then he can further push his agenda with your support. He can reward you with praise and attention and point out how "wise" you are. If you do not agree with him then he can be the "victim" and use it against you later with other people behind your back and advance his position anyway. He can also point out how "crazy" or "stupid" you are. An example would be like this: "Your Mother is being cruel to me, this is wrong, and I am right, if you agree with her you are cruel and wrong also." This thinking error is a common tactic used among narcissists to divide family members, close friends, and acquaintances. The narcissist can cause/create a conflict driven environment. That conflict rich environment helps the narcissist divide and conquer by promoting hurt feelings. The narcissist is an expert at using those perceived hurt feelings to cause further division among people who care about each other. The true evil of this thinking error is in the way the narcissist employs it. Usually he employs it in an underhanded way and secretly with others to create animosity against you. You never know the damage is done until the smoke clears. Secrecy is the method he most employs although he will also directly present you with only two choices openly if he thinks it will serve his need to control. The narcissist will often couple this thinking error with drama and emotion to block your initial thoughts on the matter and narrow your thinking down to only two options. Most situations have more than only two options; do not let the narcissist narrow your options and thus direct your choices. The narcissist loves to direct your thinking. He can only do so if you allow him to do so. If you fall into his trap it becomes a never-ending spiral of drama and poor decisions. You are doing what you think you want to do, however you are really doing what he wants you to do. Do not fall for this.

2. The closed ended question. This one is a huge red flag. The narcissist will employ the closed ended question to direct your thoughts and responses to make his point. He will do this to your friends, family and anyone he thinks will help his cause which is winning control. He is pathologically dedicated to exerting his control in your life and over all your relationships. If the question can only be answered with a "yes" or "no" answer, then you are facing a closed ended question. Suppose that your narcissist has been surfing porn sites and you expressed your

frustration with his behavior, an example of a closed ended question posed by him might be: (Narcissist) "Are you still being paranoid?" The question is a clumsy attempt for the narcissist to sidestep the issue of trust in the relationship and the co-occurring betrayal issues that you may be feeling. The closed ended question is an attempt to label you the "Paranoid" person, and eventually this label will become "crazy" rather than "paranoid." You are labeled from the start of the conversation as "paranoid" since the question is phrased as if you were paranoid in the first place. If you answer "No" then you are "admitting" you were paranoid in the past. If you answer "Yes" then you are "admitting" paranoia presently. Either way you support the narcissists' position that he is doing nothing wrong and you are just being "paranoid." This manipulation technique is classic gas lighting and a huge red flag. Besides being a classic false premise, it also inherently denies any wrongdoing on his part and invalidates your feelings. Now the issue is not the intimate betrayal involving him surfing porn sites and masturbating to nude images online. The vampire has sidestepped his hurtful behavior that damages trust and causes stress in the relationship in numerous ways. The issue as posed in the closed ended question is now "your" Paranoia. This is just standard narcissistic gas-lighting and narcissists do it at a championship level. It is just one of many ways to infer that you are "crazy." He can also move into his defense mode and make it your fault that he surfs porn sites: "If you weren't always checking up on my every move, I might trust you more." Now his emotional infidelity is your fault, due entirely to your behavior, never his behavior. His act of dishonesty, his betrayal of trust, now becomes your fault for calling him out on his distasteful, destructive, unfaithful, behavior.

3. Circular reasoning, Narcissist style: "I always tell the truth because I hate liars; since I hate liars and everyone who knows me, knows this about me, I am always truthful." The narcissist often uses the close ended question to move into circular reasoning. The best way around this game is to refuse to play. However, there are some other countermeasures although they will usually not be effective in the long run. Remember, the narcissist will defend his indefensible position to the bitter end as his ego is intertwined with his position. If his position were to fall, his ego falls with it and he will never let that happen. He will try to destroy you before he allows his ego to fall. This will be true of overt and covert narcissists. We will delve into some countermeasures later.

4. AD Hominem attack, (translated as "against the man.") This is the personal attack and it is usually directed against you or anyone who does not agree with the narcissists' position. This direct insult is usually coupled with circular reasoning and close ended questions. This personal attack will usually be used by the narcissist to attack your character rather than the facts or position you are discussing. It can also be used against you with other people by manipulating their opinion against you. Conversely it can be used to attack/manipulate other people by manipulating your opinion against them. All of this is usually done in secret however the vampire can also be overt in his attacks. With most narcissists it is a combination of overt and covert. Whenever a person's character, belief system, faith, sexuality, physical attributes, race, culture, or political affiliation is attacked rather than the merits of their position, you have the Ad Hominem fallacy.

5. The Straw Man Argument. The straw man argument is easy to recognize, and it is a narcissist favorite. He uses straw man arguments to "strengthen" his other thinking errors. Basically, it involves putting forth a position and then making an argument for that position by making an argument for (or against) a completely unrelated position. The narcissist uses the

Straw Man option when he cannot defeat your actual position/argument. He will "set up" a false, unrelated argument and "defeat or win" his own set up. When the narcissist "wins" that false/unrelated argument he will then use the "win" as a basis for proving his current position. Remember, the narcissist must win every argument by any means necessary. Do not expect logic or reason within the interaction. There will only be drama. I have had many clients who are attacked with a straw man argument. They have successfully embraced recovery and rejected the toxic culture of addiction only to be told by their pet narcopath: "You may have quit heroin, but you drink a lot of coffee. You have not quit coffee, so you are still an addict."

Some points to ponder.

Narcissistic relationships are fear-based relationships. The narcissist successfully and instinctually plays upon fears and desires. What were you looking for when you found the narcissist? People are always looking for things that give them meaning and pleasure. People search for what they desire both consciously and sub-consciously. Narcissists desire control and supply. What did you desire when you allowed the vampire into your life? People search for a lot of things, love, meaning, health, knowledge. Some people search for understanding, companionship, and peace. The most dangerous thing they search for is familiarity. People are pattern seekers, we tend to seek what we know. What was it about your chosen narcissist that was so familiar to you? We generally only know what we remember. We search out that which we remember and is familiar to us. Figuring out this dynamic is crucial to eliminating narcissists from your life forever. This is important because you will find varying degrees of narcissists everywhere. At work, within your family, at the gym, in classes. Everywhere. Recognizing their patterns will save you from the toxic enmeshment that is the drama and pain of a narcissistic relationship. What patterns did you learn in childhood? Take your time with this question.

You stayed in the narcissistic relationship because of fear. Your fears were used to manipulate you. Fear of being alone, fear of not having the security of a "relationship." Fear of being hurt or losing out. Fear of losing all you invested into the relationship. Fear of not being loved. Fear of losing love. Fears unique to you. Fear exists with desire. If you desired nothing from the relationship, there would be no fear to use as a tool for manipulation. When you think you possess something, either a person, place, or thing, fear is always in the background. The fear of losing what you either possess or want to possess. The narcissist knows instinctively what it wants out of you. The big question for you to consider is: What did you want from the narcissistic relationship? Narcissists know you want love. They know you want to make sure that you have and maintain a loving relationship. People want to love and be loved by others. This is natural for actual humans. That is where fear plays its role in the vampire relationship. The narcissist knows instinctively how to manipulate you into trying desperately to secure the "relationship." Thus, you are always insuring the vampire is fed. Once you start to do things to secure the relationship, fear is running the show. You have become enmeshed within the monster's web of deceit and manipulation. The predator is in charge. The predator is incapable of actual love. Real love requires empathy and compassion. Vampires possess neither.

The show will end however. It will end because it is toxic. It will end because it is a dynamic that cannot be sustained. Once you have sacrificed your personal freedom, dignity, and self-esteem to sustain the narcissistic relationship you might simply give up due to mental, physical, and emotional exhaustion. You might end the relationship due to sudden self-realization and radical self-honesty. You may surrender due to your own rational self-interest. You may realize with every fiber of your moral being that it is now time to heal. Surrender due to becoming emotionally unable to continue can be a strong motivator. Moving on to a better, healthier life can become a strong catalyst for new growth. The relationship will most likely end due to narcissistic discard. The vampire likes to abuse his tools.

The narcissist pathologically seeks new supply instinctively and it may find a new supply. Once that happens (and it is a frequent occurrence in a narcissistic relationships) the vampire will "monkey branch" to its new supply. This might happen with no warning. Often, it happens with a typical narcissist pattern. The narcissist will devalue you or try to destroy you before throwing you away like garbage. The narcissist will claim it is all your fault and you deserve it. He will claim victim status. In some ways the narcissistic relationship may linger on because your thinking has become impaired. Your idea of "normal" within a relationship is now based on giving away your power and allowing yourself to be used as a supply source. Some narcissistic relationships are just like being in a prison whereby you serve a life sentence on the installment plan. Breaking up and reconnecting for years. The narcissist is pathologically driven to manipulate and stay locked on to his food source. It will not let go until it has secured another food source. They use "love bombing" and "hoovering" to keep you locked in when you try to leave. Don't fall for it. Love bombing and all that comes with it are just recognizable patterns. Once you learn to recognize the patterns you are on your way to freedom.

Please remember the following:

The Narcissists motto is "I did not do that."

The Narcissists slogan is "It's never my fault, it's your fault I did that." (But I still didn't do it.)

The Narcissists oath is "I am never at fault. You asked for it, that's why I did it." ("But I still didn't do it and you're crazy for accusing me."

The goal of every narcissist when he is having a conversation, (or a conflict) is to win, never to foster understanding or to help communication. His idea is one of victory at all costs, especially cost to you.

Narcissist: Why are you always so cold to me, so paranoid and defensive? Do you have any idea why you cannot trust? You are so cruel!

You: "I am not defensive; you are always surfing online porn!"

Narcissist:" A person with no trust is always paranoid of the people who truly love them."

You: "I am not paranoid, I checked your browser history and it's loaded with porn sites!"

Narcissist: "You are always so defensive! How can anyone ever trust a paranoid person like you?" "You are incapable of true love! You violated my trust!"

Conversation with a narcissist is a steel trap of manipulation. You will never prevail with logic, truth, or reason. This is because logic, truth, and reason have no place to live inside a narcissistic relationship. If you find your conversations going like the above, you are in a dysfunctional relationship with a narcissist/abuser. No contact, or controlled contact is the way towards sanity and healing. If you value daily personal interactions filled with closed ended questions, false premises, circular reasoning, false dichotomies, false equivalencies, drama, personal attacks, gaslighting, triangulation, and overall, general deception then stay in a relationship with a narcissist. If you want to change the destructive dynamic, you must first recognize the twisted dynamic. Here are some things to pay attention to. The narcissist will use a divide and conquer strategy when it comes to your family, co-workers, social media, social acquaintances, and friends. If you find yourself in the position of having to defend and explain yourself to family, friends, co-workers, and acquaintances due to your narcissist, you are in trouble. Most likely he may have already recruited his "Flying Monkeys" to help him extract his resources from you. If you feel the need to check his search history and you feel betrayed, listen to your feelings. He will accuse you of his behavior. He will blame others and present himself as a victim. He will justify his behavior with ridiculous and un-truthful explanations.

You can keep on living in chaos and toxicity until you wake up one day and you realize that you have been in a mental prison during the relationship and you are a willing source of energy and sustenance for your chosen vampire. You have been in a prison of your own making more time than you have been free. You have cooperated with the vampire and have learned to call the monsters dungeon "home." You live in darkness and call the darkness "light."

I would like you to consider the meaning of the word "*Survival*." Webster's New World Dictionary, Third College Edition defines survival as "The act, state, or fact of surviving." It goes on to define survival as "Something or someone who survives." Researching a bit further in

Webster's we find the word *"Survive."* The definition of survive I like best is "To **continue to live after or in spite of**." The example used in Webster's Dictionary is: "To continue to live after, or in spite of, a shipwreck." If you currently in a relationship with a narcissist your life is officially a "shipwreck." You are not sailing through life, you are crashing upon the rocks of a dangerous and dysfunctional narcissistic relationship. No ship ever created can sail upon rocks and manage to remain afloat. You do not have to ability to heal, rescue, or "fix" the vampire that is draining you. No one has that ability. Your compassion and empathy will be used against you. This will be your reality as long as you allow it to remain so.

As a narcissists supply source, you have some tough challenges ahead of you. You will be challenged to survive and thrive despite your decision to become involved with a vampire/predator. You are being challenged to seek freedom despite his demented manipulation of your family, friends, society and you. Make no mistake about this fact, you are in this situation because you allow it to continue. This all came about because you allowed the chaos to grow. In some very crucial and important ways you have enabled this blood sucking parasite to drain you. This is because you have empathy, and the monster took advantage of you. Using something he lacks, and you possess, he gained a powerful tool. He used this tool for the extraction of your time, energy, and resources. Do not be ashamed for possessing innate humanity. Do not be ashamed for having compassion and empathy. This is the benchmark for being a real human. A human can control his or her instincts. An animal cannot control its instincts. An animal is ruled by its instincts. The narcissist/vampire cannot live without obtaining supply. It is pathologically driven to obtain supply. This instinct driven behavior is the vampire's weakness and this base instinct to control/consume is easily recognizable.

I am going to ask you to use your powers of imagination for a minute. What are you most afraid of and why? Take time to answer this question because the answer will provide you with something the minion of chaos uses to control you. Imagine that you can come home one day, and your narcissist/abuser is permanently gone from your life. Your house is neat, clean, and quiet. You have no accusations to face, no drama to deal with, no silent treatment, no gaslighting, and no flying monkeys attacking you. No toxic triangulations to deal with. Imagine peace. Imagine your life is no longer full of chaos anymore. No one has been violated and you feel safe within the best place on the planet for you to feel safe within, your bedroom. Instead of the nonstop demands for attention, (both negative and positive) and resource, energy draining, narcissistic drama, there is only peace. What would you do with peace? How would you feel about your goals and aspirations? How would you feel about the absence of your narcissist as opposed to his presence in your life now? Does the thought of a drama free life frighten you? This last question is very important. Only you can answer it truthfully. Only you can deal with the answer. Only you can remove the tools of the monster.

Consider this: A narcissist can wake up in the morning unemployed and broke, yet he manages to maintain a "relationship." By the end of the day he has secured the resources needed to manage his unquenchable supply needs. He has fed his massive, ever empty ego. He has done so from literally possessing nothing but his dysfunctional use of thinking errors. He uses manipulation, and a championship level ability to drain/extract your energy, time, and attention. (Both negative and positive attention.) Narcissistic thinking patterns carry within them some keen survival skills, however these skills always come at the expense of others. They always create a dysfunctional relationship between the narcissist, his supply source, and the society he lives in. *Always remember, in many ways, narcissists are perceived by society as victims needing understanding and healing. Narcissists are incapable of being rehabilitated. The common reality running through all this dynamic is that the true victims are those created by the narcissist and they need healing.*

Living with a toxic narcissist is a threat to your financial, social, and even physical survival. If you really look at things logically, living with a narcissist for any length of time is a very real threat to your continued existence as a vibrant, free, self-actualized human being. If you just take into consideration the false accusations, the toxic mental games and manipulations, you have quite enough to deal with. When you consider the co-occurring damage to your self-esteem and important relationships with others, both personal and professional, a narcissist poses serious risk factors to your life. When I was a Case Manager at Pelican Bay State Prison, I had many inmates in my anger management classes. I always knew who would learn something and who would not learn anything. The people who displayed real empathy and compassion could be reached. The others simply blamed other people, "the system," and even their victims for their current circumstances. Their instinct driven behavior was never considered as a contributing factor in their current circumstance. Many times they blamed their victims for "making" them commit violence.

Societal violence, situational violence, and manipulation rule the responses and daily life of the narcissist. This is because he is unable to communicate in any healthy or authentic manner with another human being. Communication with a Narcopath is always based on manipulation. The narcissist must achieve victory at all costs. Communication is always a competition that the narcissist must win, and you must lose. This means that if you are communicating with a narcissist, he wants you to lose, always. There is no exception to this pattern. You are in a secret competition that only he knows exists. A home with a narcissist is a small insane asylum that you really don't want to call home. Within the walls of a narcissists dwelling place you will always find drama, pain, sadness, regret, and loss. You will always find people who are unhappy and eventually drained and discarded. Living with a narcissist will only help make social violence, situational violence, manipulation, and self-doubt a daily fact of life within a psychological prison you helped co-create. The relationship with the narcissist is based upon false mental constructs. False constructs designed and used by the predator to create dysfunctional relationships between yourself and people you care about. The vampire will not be content with just gaining some control because the narcissist's daily thoughts are dominated by thoughts of total control. Always co-occurring with perceived power or lack thereof. The narcissist must drain its supply. These realities of narcissistic feeding are all toxic constructs that you allow into your life. The narcissist can never gain enough control to satisfy his toxic instincts. Everyone is a tool to him and he always uses his tools much too recklessly and much too hard. He (or she) eventually destroys what it feeds upon. You are allowing the vampire to feed.

The first challenge for you to attempt is the challenge of overcoming the false mental constructs the narcissist assumes (and demands) that you accept. Subtle or blatant, overt or covert, the narcissist will always be driven to consume energy. This is the reality brought on by the unnatural pathology inherent within the narcissists thinking processes. Life with a narcissist demands an acceptance of narcissistic domination by the victims themselves. Victims of narcissistic abuse unwittingly reinforce the narcissist's abilities to feed upon them just by accepting the terms of living together. The victim adapts over time to the toxic culture of narcissistic abuse. Your first challenge is to consider the false constructs of your pet narcissist and how your very core identity conflicts with the narcissists opinions of how you "should" be in the world. The vampire's views are always correct and paramount to anyone else's views. If you allow it, he will harm your interactions with society, your relationships with people you love, and even your self-esteem. The narcissist wants to cut you off from major life experiences, so he can have all your energy, resources, and time to himself. He will attempt to stop you from meeting and experiencing healthy people, places, and things. In your professional life he will try to destroy your interactions with people who might have become friends, mentors, and guides. I simply cannot stress this point enough: Being in a relationship with a narcissist can harm work place relationships, and even impact your own family members. The entire relationship with a Narcopath is always based on false constructs. As you regain control of your life and happiness and you re-engage with life once again you will have insights. The first healthy insight is when you finally accept that it is time to let the narcissist go.

You are much more than the deranged projections, thinking errors, and manipulations of your abuser. You are a child of an unlimited universe, and the narcissist can only limit you if you allow him or her to do so. Remember who you are. You are not your "culture," you are not your "race," you are not your "family." You are not the beliefs and expectations of others. You are the universe out picturing itself as you. You are more than a label. You are more than "Straight," "Transgender," "Gay," "Lesbian," "Male," or "Female." You are much more than a "color." You are much greater and magical than you know. You will find that Narcopaths tend to hold extreme views. Many abusive people are extremely intolerant towards others. Toxic racists are natural abusers. Whenever you find hatred based on race, culture, sexual orientation, politics, or fake polarities that do not actually exist, you often find severe narcissists. It is time for you to learn who you really are. Once you know and truly accept the truth of your being, there will be no room for narcissistic predations. You will no longer be manipulated by the polarizing language of savages. You will again join the Human family. You will leave the vampires behind. All of us register somewhere unique on the color chart of the universe. There are no mistakes. We are an expression of a sure and sacred tonal range. I use this spoken word expression with my clients who are struggling with being labeled and insulted because of their race, sex, or gender expression. I hope it can be of use to you also.

Consider this: (From one of my spoken word poems entitled "Earthtribe.")

I must tell you the tale of our true Mother. The Mother of the Earthtribe, I must tell you who first birthed Her (our Mother) and how she came into being. I must tell you all about the Mother of our Mother. And within the telling, you will learn about the first Mother, our Great-Grandmother **Source,** and within this learning you will discover a long-hidden truth: We are all one tribe, The Earthtribe.

Once upon a time there existed Source, a Source of all that is and ever will be; a Source that exists always, even right now, even after Source existed. For this is the sacred mystery held within the Source of The All. Many have tried to name, classify, and identify Source but all have failed for Source just is and Source will always be, and Source has no name. Source is un-nameable for Source exists within a thought form that is not word connected thought nor dependent upon symbols and is thus unlimited. Source is powerful and mysterious for even the word "unlimited" cannot describe a limitless existence, and all attempts to describe the freedom of Source limits the understanding of Source, for Source cannot be contained by such descriptions. Source can only be experienced, and never can this experience of Source be explained by those it creates. Source cannot be touched but that which comes from Source can be touched and touch others, although all things from Source come and go, and always transform and sometimes they transform into the untouchable, only to be touched again.

Source cannot die as it can only transform, and it can only create, for Source is sacred and thus mysterious, and as we all know, anything truly sacred is beyond word-connected thought and thus beyond thought-form understanding. Thus, sacred texts will always fail to encompass The All and usually lead to extremism and chaos. Everything created by Source cannot die, only transform just like Source, for everything is in Source's image which is The All. Source can be glimpsed within the space between atoms and molecules, for Source not only forms the space, it is the space, the vibration, and the attraction between them. Yet even this is not **the all** of Source, only an observable aspect of Source for those who pay attention to such things.

Sometimes the creative force of Source looks like destruction to earth-bound minds, but this is only because Source is not bound by space or time. Vibrational rates are a manifestation of Source, but they are not Source. Some name Source "Void" and this symbol-creation works well also. For everything indeed comes from Void and everything returns to Void and The All has already been created only to cycle and be re-created endlessly within endless forms. This is the sacred mystery of how Source first created the Sacred Mother of our Sacred Mother and how the Earthtribe was first created. By Source alone came The All, thus Source is The All. This is unknowable however I still call Source "Great-Grandmother." Many within the Earthtribe do so as well. We seem to like this designation for it sooths a temporarily earthbound mind.

Source cares not about race nor wealth, or national and religious pride, or sports heroes, actresses, actors, singers, talk show hosts, or war, or social position, or belief, or lack of belief, for Source creates only free will creation and those things are all created in turn by those expressions first created by Source. Source just is and can be experienced but never explained, controlled, understood, or codified. We who are created by Source have created time in our own image. Using this beautiful and practical illusion we have dated the universe brought into being by Source at 13.7 billion years old.

*Source however, is beyond time but we carefully ignore this fact for this is also soothing to a temporarily earthbound mind. Since we are the creators of time as we understand time, we count these numbers as correct for we have created the numbers also, even though numbers and time cannot contain nor explain Source. As beings from Source we are creators also and thus we can create a Heaven or Hell or anything in between. We can also create realities beyond Heaven or Hell however we don't realize this yet. We will. Some have named Source "The Big Bang" however this is only an emanation from the Void and thus cannot be Source, only an example of something coming into being from the Void, something that will eventually return to the Void. Something of Source and not actually Source. It is simply **The Heartbeat of Source.*** A limitless heartbeat that will continue creating endlessly. We experience the pause between beats and then reason the pause to be the totality of existence when it is simply something coming into being. *The sacred truth of "Being-Becoming" that few can understand, much less translate from its original Sanskrit.*

We, born from the Earth Mother that our Primordial Mother Source first created and gave birth to, (only one of uncountable Mothers within uncountable multi-verses) thus in turn creating Her, the source of Us, seek always to understand and even (rather stupidly) to interpret, comprehend, and master Source for we can sense the celestial knowledge within Source even if we cannot comprehend it. Since Source exists in a realm far beyond word connected thought, the word "master" means nothing to Source and is only a creation from the many new Creators that Source brings froth via Void. This is all a fool's errand but a noble enterprise within our current, collective evolution and transformational process.

We only need to experience Source and with that experience will come enough understanding, however we do not, as a species, quite understand all this yet. We will. For one day we will transform. One day we will realize that we are only one tribe, the Earthtribe, and that it is impossible to be separate from our collective Source. We are One. We are The All. We are Source and she is Us for we all were born from the same Source. There is no duality, no separation from Source or from each other. We are Earthtribe, Planetary Citizens, but also

Universal Citizens and Multi-versal Citizens. We are made of everything the uncountable galaxies are constructed of. All else that contradicts this self-evident truth must one day be seen for what it is, Maya/illusion and it is all self-perpetrated for we create it all. If you think we are separate remember Fukashima, remember the Pacific Ocean, for it is transforming before your eyes. We are one planet, one people, and there is no back yard. Anywhere.

Source gave our universe what it needed to create for this is what Source always does. Using created thought forms, we have named the un-nameable gifts that Source has continually bestowed upon us. Strong and weak nuclear forces, gravitational pull, the elemental table, electro-magnetic forces, and all created from the dust left over by exploding stars. Using our word-connected thought form created numbers, we estimate the Earth Mother to have begun cooling around 4.6 billion years ago, and all reckoned in our self-created time even though we know time has no actual reckoning. We have proven this, yet we cannot at this time overcome our self-imposed limitations in order to transcend our current self-imposed, duality driven, developmental level.

Gasses came into being for they were needed in order to create Her. Hydrogen, helium, carbon dioxide, water vapor, ammonia, oxygen, all came from Source and we in turn created what we needed to understand as best we can in our current transformation these precious gifts from

Source. (We have however, missed the sacred mystery in so doing.) Gravitational pull brought into being stars, planets and their orbiting moons, meteors, comets, asteroids, and all forms thus needed for life to begin within. The many creations from Source coalesced together to create in turn their own creations, for this is the sacred nature, miracle, and true mystery of Source. The essence of the creator is always found within all that is created, and this is why it is easy to know the deception of duality once you experience Source. What is within is also without. That which is above is also below. Sometimes that which seems evil is good and that which seems good is evil. Discernment helps the earthbound mind when it comes to duality.

The primordial Mother of the Earthtribe Mother (Source's daughter, one of uncountable daughters within uncountable multi-verses) obviously loved water, for she was originally covered in it. We (the children of her child) in turn are made from it. Our tears remind us of Her for they still carry the primordial salts of her being. We are truly stardust water beings just as she is, for we are constructed of all that is Her. This is the nature of Source. This is the nature of The All. This is unknowable.

About 3.5 billion years ago, calculated using our thought form symbols which meant nothing during that transformation for we had not created time yet, Primordial Earth Mother (Grandmother) brought forth her first young, creating as she in turn was created, always following the prime directive of Source as all must do even when they refuse to do so. For even in refusing to follow Source one still does the will of Source, for The All works to the benefit of Source regardless. This is unstoppable because Source always is and always does and cannot do anything other than create that which creates. These single celled organisms led to multi-celled organisms and about 750 million years ago plants and animals began to come into being, for true growth is always transformation and always grows more and more complex.

Again, time meant nothing 750 million years ago for we were not there yet to create time in our own image and thus install limits upon existence. Source is beyond time always and thus acts outside of time always and as such is limitless. Though we use mental constructs to glimpse Source we do not define Source for our mental constructs cannot yet do this. The All will simply not fit within our mental and psychological creations even though they are of The All. Within the inherent limitations of the symbolic thought form we call language many have become temporarily lost and thus conclude that there is no free will. This is incorrect for Source encompasses more than can be understood within a symbolic thought form. That which leads to thought leads to freedom but that which leads to thought can also lead to thought forms that lead in turn to chains; mental, spiritual, and physical. That which leads to Source will lead one beyond word connected thought and once therein one finds answers and acceptance. Since this process is unknowable it remains a mystery to many, though secretly known by some. Usually the innocent, for they are not fond of duality and do not like to dwell within the socially/economically/theoretically/racially and falsely created two camp continuums of "them" and "us." For the innocent are born knowing that there is no "them" and there is no "us" there is only the All.

About 150,000 years ago our Mother was born from Her Mother, Earth. Our collective Mother knew nothing of time for time was not yet invented and thus meant nothing. She knew of cycles, sun cycles, moon cycles, her sacred cycles, and the cycles of plants and animals, though the concept of "animal" was not yet in vogue. One of Mother's children, Rebecca Cann, being a creator herself and thus creating in turn, in her Earth Mother's image, chose to devote herself to science, the study of DNA, and the pursuit of knowledge. For this is what those who create do, they always pursue knowledge. They seek the fountainhead of Source for this is a prime directive. If you listen.

She and others listened for they knew that listening facilitates learning. This Earth Sister and her Earth Brother Allen Wilson, mapping DNA and using matrichronology have shown that all human lines trace back to the ovaries of a single Mother, brought forth by Earth Mother around 150,000 years ago. Using our newly created symbol-language we have named the place of Her birth "Africa." We are Her children. Our Father was called "Adamu" by some and this meant "Son of the Red Mother Earth." Other researchers are tracing his trail even as I write this for you. The DNA markers of our primordial parents are carried within our sacred and magical bloodlines. Our very lifeblood sings this ancient and truly magical song of creation. **We are One People. We are one tribe. We are Earthtribe.** And we have forgotten this. We must remember, for it is this sacred truth can save us all.

Our Earth Sister Rebecca Cann collected DNA from other Sisters, Sisters from Asia, Europe, the South pacific, Americans from African descendants, and her Earth Brother in science, Mark Stoneking, collected DNA from other Earth Sisters also, aboriginal Australians and New Guineans. They published their results in the magazine Nature and in so doing proved that we are all children of the Earthtribe, and we are all related. We all come from Our Mother, the collective Mother. **The One**. She was a child of Mother Earth, our Grandmother, created in turn from Source, Our Great-Grandmother, and We are Her and She is Us for it is impossible to be separate from Source. We are One People. The People of Earth. We are a planetary tribe. The Earth is Our collective home. We are Earthtribe. Look around and see Source in everyone and know that we must cease killing one another and hating one another for when we kill each other we truly murder our own brothers and sisters. When we hate each other, we hate our own family, our own tribe, our own mother. We hate ourselves.

We hate what we see reflected in the eyes of those we hate.

Feeling worthless because of cultural labels, sexual orientation, or blatant racism is a false narcissistic construct. Narcissistic abuse encourages and enforces hatred and division. This is not the core truth of your being. This false construct ignores the magic of your actual existence. The miracle inherent within life. There is no separation in the tribe of earth except the false and toxic separations we construct. There is nothing more Narcopathic than to be "proud" of your "race" while hating others because of their "race." No one picks their "race" and it is cruel to hate people because of the tonal range they were born with. The miracle within being part of the human race must be celebrated and acknowledged. Predators have their role in existence for they make us stronger. It is our duty to overcome their predations. The Narcopath either cannot or will not see the sacred magic in humanity. However, that tragedy must sadly remain his toxic reality alone, for you do not deserve such cruel insanity. No one does. Once you recognize the vampire, you can deal with the vampire. You will one day realize your strength and you will be thankful for the lessons. When you can thank the vampire for the lessons and move on without hatred, you are no longer under its power and control. Hatred is something that co-occurs with fear. When you have become fear-less, you are no longer available as energy-food for the vampire. This state of being will take some time and effort on your part. Within the toxic relationship you had little control over this false construct that was invented, created, and constantly reinforced by the narcissist-vampire. This is because you were unable to recognize the sick game he was playing. You possess empathy, this is normal for humans, he had no compassion. He had thinking errors, logical fallacies, and toxic manipulations. Learning to see the false constructs of the narcissist is a rebirth back into life and society. Reconsider the narcissistic relationship for the false construct it is. Toxic narcissism will not foster the new growth that the universe is demanding of you at this time. Malignant intolerance is a red flag for narcissism.

"Remember, your chosen affirmation should be the last thing you say to yourself as you are falling asleep and the first thought on your mind when you wake up each morning."

If you have avoided being destroyed by the vampire thus far then you are to be commended because you are a survivor. You may not have considered making it through the narcissistic relationship as a survival challenge, but it is a survival challenge. You have a powerful skill for you have proven that you can adapt and survive. Survival is a matter of gaining the skills you need and recognizing the skills you have at your disposal. It is also a matter of considering new information and adapting to change. Changes in perception can require the letting go of old, outdated patterns of being within the world. Stop lying to yourself if you are doing life on the installment plan with a toxic narcissistic vampire. Stop feeding the dysfunctional beast. *Start thinking like a survivor.*

Suggestions:

Go to your local library or go online and look up books on narcissism. Is your narcissist violent? Is the narcissist abusing drugs or alcohol? What is the dynamic you are surviving under right now? You must be honest about your current survival situation. If you continue to allow the mental and/or physical abuse and toxic environment to dominate your life, your physical and mental well-being will suffer. Your loved ones will suffer along with you. *They suffer when you suffer.* Your children also learn about relationships from your relationships. Remember that fact.

Think about and answer the following question:

How does my current relationship affect my life?

You should include in your answer what you want out of life, what you want for your family and those who care about you. Remember to be honest about your current situation. If this is a romantic relationship or a relationship with members of your family, make sure to include these challenges within your considerations. If you can write this out, please do so however make sure that the narcissist will never see it or have access to it. If you can write this out it is important to write this out because you need to slow down your thoughts and start developing a plan for thriving and not just surviving. Don't worry about being perfect the first time around. Online forums on narcissistic abuse are also good places to process your feelings and insights. You can do this anonymously, and depending on the level of toxicity, make sure your narcissist cannot access your account or your electronic devices. *Just relax, take a deep breath and write.*

Remember that you are more than just your past, more than just your current relationship. More than your culture, sexual identity, and more than your "race." You are more than just your interactions with people, places, and things. You are a human being. Your past only defines you if you allow it to do so. *You are much more than your past.* You only have control over today, but remember, you are a timeless being, you are the universe out picturing itself and you are created from all that created the cosmos. You deserve better. "*We are truly stardust water beings.*"

Chapter One Personal Development Questions:

Do you have a favorite holiday that means more to you than any other holiday?

Why is this holiday so meaningful to you?

How has narcissistic abuse affected your life?

How will this toxic dynamic hinder your new growth?

Remember this earlier example? Reconsider it, seriously reconsider it:

"The first challenge for you to attempt is the challenge of overcoming the false mental constructs the narcissist arrogantly assumes you will accept. Subtle or blatant, overt or covert, the narcissist will always be driven to consume your energy. This is the reality brought on by the unnatural toxicity inherent within the narcissist's instinct driven, predatory thinking processes. Life with a narcissist demands an acceptance of narcissistic domination by the victims themselves. Victims of narcissistic abuse unwittingly (or sometimes willingly) reinforce the narcissist's abilities to feed upon them just by accepting the terms of living together. Your first challenge is to consider the false constructs of your pet narcissist and how your very core identity conflicts with the narcissists opinions of how you "should" be in the world. His views are always correct and paramount to anyone else's views. If you allow it, he will harm your interactions with society, your relationships with people you love, and even your self-esteem. The narcissist wants to cut you off from major life experiences, so he can have all your energy, resources, and time to himself. He will attempt to stop you from meeting and experiencing beautiful people, places, and things. In your professional life he will try to destroy your interactions with people who might have become friends, mentors, and guides. Being in a relationship with a narcissist can harm work place relationships, and even impact your own family members. The entire relationship with a narcissist is always based on false constructs. As you regain control of your life and happiness and you re-enter life and society once again, it is time to let the narcissist go. However first you must let his projections, thinking errors, false constructs, and dishonesty go by the wayside. You must realize the truth of your being. You are much more than the deranged projections, thinking errors, and manipulations of your narcissist. You are much more than just a food source to a vampire. You are a child of an unlimited universe, and the narcissist can only limit you if you allow him (or her) to do so.

Chapter One Affirmations:

I am the child of a beneficent universe and as such I am a universal being. Growth is my prime directive.

I enjoy setting healthy goals and I enjoy accomplishing them.

I enjoy setting healthy boundaries.

I am open to communication with healthy people.

I choose happiness.

Chapter Two

Choices

If you are reading this book, then you are most likely in a toxic or abusive relationship. You may suspect that you are involved with someone who is a Narcopath. Perhaps you are concerned about a parental or family relationship. It might be a married relationship or a love interest. You may also be a concerned family member or friend of someone who is currently suffering narcissistic abuse. You may feel abused in some ways right along with them. As such you may be seeking answers that will help both of you. I advise you to not think of this book as another "program." Mental health systems love "programs." There are work programs, tough love programs, even warm and fuzzy programs like working with puppies and listening to audio books. After almost twenty years of working with prisoners, violent offenders, addicts, and parolees I know one thing all too well. **Programs generally fail.** I have seen addicts, prisoners and parolees fail in program after program. I have also seen addicts, prisoners, and parolees with no programs succeed. Attitude trumps a program every time. I have seen this repeatedly. *Your current situation in life has very little to do with your success or failure in life.* Your attitude is the best predictor of success. Right now you may see no way out of the abusive relationship. That is OK because one day can make a huge difference in your life. The important thing is to cultivate an attitude of possibility. Believe that you can make healthy change. Accept that positive possibilities exist.

This book is a resource, a guide, a map to a new way of thinking and being in the world. Use this as a workbook to grow in new, healthy, life affirming directions. Think of this book as an attitude adjuster. You are at a crossroads now; you cannot live the old way and not bring suffering into your life. You cannot live the old way and not bring suffering into the lives of those who care about you. The best way to change your old way of being in the world is to grow in a new direction. The best way to grow in a new direction is to examine your thoughts, thinking processes, your expectations, and your assumptions about the world you live in. Your assumptions about the relationships you choose to engage in may need a fresh examination.

Old, outdated, dangerous thoughts become old, outdated, negative habits. New, positive, life affirming thoughts transform over time into new, positive, life affirming habits. It is your task to unmask the malignant rituals that have become the abusive relationship. This will take effort on your part. It took time for the vampire to find your weaknesses in order to exploit them and feed upon your energy. The vampire studied you carefully, so it could recognize and avoid your strengths. The toxic relationship was cemented over time until it became accepted. It took concentrated repetition on your part for those old, outdated, negative thoughts to become dangerous, freedom crushing habits. You will have to put in the work to change your thinking, but the rewards are **AWESOME.** You will have to **choose** to grow in new directions. You have the innate ability to replace **every** one of your negative habits with positive habits. *You are what you choose to become. You can become a changed person if that is what you truly desire.*

Getting free from the vampire is just a passing thought right now. Absent healthy choices, the word "Freedom" is only a group of meaningless letters. Without you making a conscious decision to seriously attempt positive change freedom is impossible. Growth can be a painful process. You may have to release some familiar people, places, and things from your old life. It may be time to let go of toxic relationships that you have become comfortable holding onto. Survival can be painful, and no one ever said survival is a painless process. Right now, the narcissist has its boot upon your neck. You can lie about your situation or you can get that boot off your neck. This will require an attitude adjustment. It is all your **CHOICE.**

A survivor does not expect others to make her/his survival choices. A survivor does not expect others to do the survival work for him or her. *All you need you have already*, it springs from your heart and it's called desire. Desire leads to choices and those choices guide your life. You make them in the present moment, moment to moment, and these choices out-picture as your future. *What does your past look like*? It is the result of your choices made within a past, long gone, present moment. Your past reflects the impact of those choices made inside former present moments that have now passed on. You can deny this but that is just your ego talking to you. The ego is always trying to make you right and everyone else wrong. You can blame your past, your culture, your religion, your race, someone else's race, your upbringing, and the Narcopath. As the abusive relationship continues you can blame the therapist, parents, flying monkeys, friends, friends of friends, and your siblings. The blame game is perfect in it's ability to deflect responsibility, because *it does not change anything regarding your choices*. Your desires led to choices and those choices have guided and impacted your life. If you refuse to admit this fact of life then you know your ego is in charge, not you. Just like the narcissist in your life, your negative life lessons will simply be repeated until learned. The ego will teach you nothing until you learn to lose your ego and begin to **choose for yourself to live a life with purpose.**

How do you choose to live a life with purpose?

First you must find the answers to four timeless and perfect questions hidden deep within yourself. These are the questions of childhood curiosity. These are questions the Narcopath will never ask himself because he fears the answers. An instinct driven animal is incapable of asking these questions authentically because they require compassion, honesty, accountability, and introspection. I am not asking you to answer these questions right now. I am just asking you to consider them, look at them, and file them away for your subconscious mind to work on throughout your life. These are the basic human questions we are all born with:

1. *Who am I?*

2. *What is my purpose?*

3. *What is the meaning of life?*

4. *Is there life after death?*

The answers to these questions will affect all your future choices. The answers to these questions lead to the only true freedom there is: *living a life of purpose*. The narcissist has only one instinct driven purpose, to feed upon others. To feed upon you he must control you by controlling your choices. Toxic manipulation is his method. His life purpose is to drain energy from his victim. His purpose is to find a supply source and latch on to it until he needs to pathologically discard his supply. These questions and their answers are crucial for your continued freedom.

They are crucial for your success or failure on freeing yourself from the narcissistic/abusive relationship. An authentic life filled with purpose cannot fail. A life without purpose has failed before it started. We will address these questions a little later. Until then, keep them in the back of your mind and let your subconscious work on them a bit. Please remember that the narcissist will never honestly address these questions within his own life. The vampire will never let you address these questions with him in any authentic manner. The vampire will not tolerate anything that might liberate his supply source from his toxic hunger. All communication with a narcissist is a contest for him to win. The abuser is only concerned with manipulation and victory at your expense. These questions are for you only. Only your answers matter. This is your first exercise in developing a healthy selfishness. This is your first exercise in developing your own rational self-interest. Your answers to these questions are your personal acknowledgment of your humanity.

The longer you stay in relationship with the narcissist the longer your basic humanity will be under constant assault. This is a natural consequence of the narcissistic abuse process. It is a very observable, predictable process. The vampire pathology depends upon thinking errors and toxic, competitive communication filled with common logical fallacies. To survive in the narcissistic relationship of toxic thinking errors, and negativity you gained an important survival skill: **Denial.** Victims of narcissistic abuse become experts in denial. Almost as good as narcissists. Vampires are pathological, and instinct driven however. Humans can observe and eventually control their instincts. This is what separates us from the primates. Psychologically you had to deny your lack of power and choice in your day to day life as a prisoner within the narcissistic/abusive relationship. Your ability to influence and change your circumstances was severely impaired. Rather than admit your powerlessness you lived in denial. You had no choice in how truthful the narcissist was being with you or others. You gradually accepted what you had to accept. You had no choice in counseling, you took what you could get. You read the books that were approved by your narcissist (If you were allowed this freedom at all.) You came to accept the toxic gas lighting. You watched only "narcissist approved" movies. If you chose and watched any program on TV it was most likely accompanied by toxic, opinionated, narcissistic chatter. You watched only "Narcissist approved" channels and shows. You had to be your own social media censor while he could freely flirt and triangulate to his toxic hearts content. Social media became less about you interacting with others in a constructive way and more about the vampire's nefarious activities online. You experienced not only a psychological **lack of freedom**, you experienced **freedom from choice**. You became used to *freedom from choice*; you began to think it was *freedom of choice*. You became accustomed to the narcissistic relationship lifestyle. You became an expert in looking the other way when it came to your true feelings. You accepted self-doubt as your new "Normal."

The vampire's opinion was the only one that mattered. You walked on eggshells and perceived it as soft sand. Denial became a coping mechanism and you became an expert in its daily use. You were surviving in the abusive environment and dying simultaneously. Your soul paid the cost.

During your period of abusive relationship captivity nothing was off limits to the narcissist. Sex (or the lack of sex) was always used as a weapon or tool for manipulation. You sometimes realized that your narcissist was a stranger that you had lived with intimately. You felt that you had to let them inspect your every feeling, opinion, and thought for approval. You became used to providing energy, both positive and negative, as a source of narcissistic supply for your live-in vampire. You found yourself doing, saying, and believing in things you never thought possible.

On the inside you searched around for answers. You sometimes "blamed" yourself and accepted the narcissist's lies as truth. You took the explanations they manipulated you with and you changed some things around. You did this, so you could make his narcissistic lies and infectious pathology more palatable. You talked endlessly with yourself about your lack of self- respect and personal honor, all the while maintaining a false front around people. Your internal dialog was self-torture. Your life was a tragic pantomime and you willingly wore the mask. All the while you were living in championship level **denial**. Accountability was not yet a consideration.

You had no personal privacy, no respect, and no personal honor. You were powerless to do anything other than submit to the will of the narcissist and you thought you would eventually "Change him." *You couldn't buy a cup of coffee, go work out, read a self-help book or have a moment for yourself without the permission of your "significant other," but you had "Peace."* He could do anything he desired. He could break all social rules and not worry if he got caught. The vampire always had the Narcopathic thinking errors to fall back on. His go to, venomous, explanations. It will always be someone else's fault. The narcissist will always play the victim. There will always be ridiculous excuses and justifications for the narcissist's behavior. Word salad will become the normal conversation. It will all make sense to the narcissist. It will be chaos for anyone interacting with the narcissist. Your life with the abuser was a living hell but you came to accept its terms. The vampire was well fed every day.

The goal of every narcissist when he is having a conversation, (or a conflict) is to win. His intention is never to foster understanding or to help communication. His idea is one of victory at all costs, especially cost to you. He must win to secure his supply. The vampire must manipulate to exist. I don't believe this pathology is one that can be changed for the better.

This abuse came at a price of course. It was personally and relationally expensive for you. None of the interaction with your pet vampire ever had a chance of fostering mutual respect. Malicious communication can never enhance your personal freedom, or personal power. Unhealthy, malignant interactions are not good for anyone. The frightening reality about destructive communication is how quickly it becomes "normal" within abusive relationships. You were only choosing from the finite and limited choices you had allowed yourself to choose from. You did not have **freedom of choice,** you had **freedom from choice**. You were in denial, and you were *powerless.* You couldn't even allow yourself an opinion for fear of "triggering" the vampire. You were afraid to speak out because you were too busy walking on eggshells around the monster you slept with. Afraid to communicate, and afraid of not being able to communicate left you paralyzed. Afraid to disagree yet ashamed to not disagree kept you isolated. Afraid to ask for intimacy while being afraid and ashamed of intimacy with the vampire kept you confused. Afraid you would be denied intimacy kept you needy. Not even animals live like that. Your ego, using **denial**, helped you survive and tolerate the narcissistic abuse. Instead of seeing the reality of your unmanageable life and unwise relationship choices, you just convinced yourself that were "Empathic." It was more acceptable to fool yourself into believing that your personal vampire "needed" you. It made the abuse somehow tolerable to fool yourself into thinking that "deep down" he was just a poor, helpless little victim. His "Inner child" was damaged and he had low self-esteem. It was all someone else's fault that he was "that" way. The vampire just needed "healing." You became his willing victim. You obeyed and accepted the "opinions" of a monster and you lived in fear. His self-created narcissistic drama drained your energy. You fed him willingly. You agreed to be his supply until he eventually decided that he would discard you for another supply. This was your un-negotiated negative contract with the vampire. Don't feel bad about it. This is everyone's negative contract with their chosen vampire. The contract stays valid until cancelled. Is it time to cancel yours?

You became involved with a toxic Narcissist because you came to accept the toxic culture of narcissism. Every victim needs their oppressor and you chose yours.

Remember:

The Narcissists motto is "I did not do that."

The Narcissists slogan is "It's never my fault, it's your fault (or someone else's fault) I did that." (But I still didn't do it.)

The Narcissists oath is "I am never at fault. You asked for it, that's why I did it." ("But I still didn't do it and you're crazy for accusing me."

You learned to protect yourself at the expense of your self-esteem and personal dignity by catering to the toxic demands of your chosen personal vampire. It is often difficult to take responsibility for your choices or decisions. If you are to heal from those choices, you must be accountable for your choices. Healing requires developing insight. Insight demands personal accountability. You learned to obey the vampire-manipulator, now learn to starve the monster.

YOU WERE CHOOSING FROM THE LIMITED CHOICES YOU THOUGHT YOU HAD PERMISSION TO CHOOSE FROM.

PRIVACY is something taken for granted by people with healthy boundaries. To invade the privacy of a mentally healthy person can incite intense disapproval. Invasion of privacy is seen as a serious transgression of healthy personal boundaries. It is often met with consequences for the boundary violator. Over the unstoppable march of time, the victims of narcissists gradually accept privacy violations. They do this because they feel that they have no **choice** in the matter. In a narcissistic relationship the conditioning can have taken years to implement. This is especially true with narcissistic parents and/or siblings. As a child with narcissistic parents this is especially damaging. The child willingly gives up choice and accepts the parent's decisions because they depend upon the narcissistic parent for survival. This sets up a lasting and toxic dynamic that is difficult to address. However, once you identify the abusive vampire patterns you can achieve freedom. It is your choice to be free. This is dependent upon you finally accepting that you have choice in the matter.

You learned many things with the abuser. You learned about gas lighting, because it happened to you daily. You learned that your feelings meant nothing because you were trained to feel that way. You learned about triangulation because you had to. *You came to accept this limited and unpleasant world view the way all people in toxic circumstances come to accept what they do not like; **gradually***. Living in **denial** you gradually learned to accept your lack of control and choice. *You finally became a source of supply and lost your sense of self. You accepted invalidation and no longer saw yourself as an authentic person*. If you do not learn to see things as they are you will stay deceived. If you fail to see how choices are important and how they make change happen over time, you will live as a prisoner to your abuser. If you stay in denial and a slave to your narcissist, always questioning yourself and accepting the toxic narcissistic dynamic, *you will surrender control of your own life to a parasite*. The universe is challenging you to step up now. You are being called to accept personhood, take the challenge. Recognize that gaining awareness of the patterns inherent within the vampire's sickness is an opportunity to gain freedom. Rejecting the creature and it's co-occurring chaos is not a punishment. Free yourself. You are worth it. Allow the minions of chaos to return to their source.

Allowing your personal vampire to rule your choices leads only to despair. Everyone else (especially you) will always be wrong and the creature will always be right. You will lose every battle and lose the ultimate war for your freedom. If you do not learn to identify and address the toxic thinking errors (both his and yours) that led to the malignant narcissist taking over your life, you are doomed to repeat the lesson. Even when you are free of

the narcissistic vampire, you will be still be imprisoned within your own mind. You will think like a victim and act like a victim. You will eventually return to the place where victims live out their lives. A world of pathological liars, narcissistic abuse, and championship level sociopaths. All of it will reflect your choices.

CHOOSE WISELY.

The major source of narcissistic abuse without exception is simple. You choose to accept the dysfunctional dynamic. You choose to not follow your instincts or listen to your inner voice for guidance. You ignored the big, red, flags. The narcissistic, manipulative thinking errors, polished by years of practice, have hijacked your world view. When choosing to heal you will be faced with decisions. Many new choices will present themselves. You may have lost the ability to see the positive possibilities within those choices. Years of **freedom from choice** may have left you unable to cope with **freedom of choice**. To reach this severely impaired dynamic you had to believe that you had no choice. Hopelessness may have invaded your soul. You always have a choice. The real question is about your readiness to change. If you are ready to change you must also be ready to recognize the consequences of past choices. This process is how we learn to make better decisions. Readiness to change is powerful.

You need to learn how to be in the world again. You must re-learn what it is to be a truly free man or woman in society post vampire. You will have to learn it from the ground up. You start by making healthy, pro-active choices. Small choices at first as these will lead to other, more important choices later. Inside the abusive relationship dynamic of narcissistic culture, you learned to be **reactive** rather than pro-active. You learned to react impulsively to the many negative situations that seem to spring up uninvited all around you. You became conditioned to relational chaos. Chaos is the natural environment of the monster you allowed into your life. If you were raised by Narcopathic parents chaos became your reality. Thus you naturally sought it out in future relationships. Your hypothalamus was always engaged in the "fight or flight" response. The chemical cascade was always just around the corner, ready to flood your brain, body, and bloodstream with the proteins and peptides needed for stress and fear. Your sympathetic nervous system and adrenal-cortical system were constantly engaged. You never realized that your own acceptance and uninformed choices put you into the many situations you were reacting too. Nor did you realize that new, healthy choices could separate you from those situations imposed upon you by the vampire. You must begin practicing being pro-active rather than re-active. You do this by making healthy choices. Healthy choices will help your body and brain. Healthy choices can give your poor, over-stimulated hypothalamus a much-needed break. Your choices can change your life, positively or negatively. *Change will always happen because of choices.*

Remember:

The Narcissists motto is "I did not do that."

The Narcissists slogan is "It's never my fault, it's your fault (or someone else's fault) I did that." (But I still didn't do it.)

The Narcissists oath is "I am never at fault. You asked for it, that's why I did it." ("But I still didn't do it and you're crazy for accusing me."

The rules in a free, healthy relationship are very different than the rules in a vampire driven relationship. Rational self-interest rules healthy choices. Your best chance for real survival is to think, consider, and choose wisely before you react to anything your narcissist creates. The abuser always manipulates relational situations for the dual purpose of controlling you and using you for narcissistic supply. Survivors do not lie about their tactical situation. Denial was just a survival game your ego came up with to help you survive the toxic prison that was your narcissistic relationship. In a free-thinking world denial is just a fancy way to lie to yourself. Using your mind correctly is your best tool in your quest for wholeness. Choosing wisely will help you create better outcomes after your vampire is gone. Being ready to make healthy change will help you thrive within the new, free world you choose to create for yourself. *You must learn to use your mind differently*. Denial helped you cope with the hopelessness and ugliness of a vampire driven life. Denial can also destroy any chance of true happiness in a world loaded with **freedom of choice**. *You must discard that old, outdated, ego driven survival skill of denial left over from your life placating and feeding a toxic vampire.* You must replace that skill with a new, free world survival skill, **Self-Honesty**. Self-honesty is a requirement of being pro-active and accountable. Remember these questions? Answer the following personal development questions and take all the time you need: (I added another one.)

1. *Who am I?*

2. *What is my purpose?*

3. *What is the meaning of life?*

4. *Is there life after death?*

5. **What does freedom mean to you?** *(I don't mean just escaping the vampire; I mean living as a free person.)*

For some people the narcissistic relationship dynamic has become a habitual way of life. This abusive dysfunction has become an accepted way of being in the world. This can be due to narcissistic parents, family members, siblings, or intense relationships of any kind. To change your past way of life you must invalidate it by growing in new directions. You can no longer tolerate old relationships that place your personal freedom, expression, and happiness in danger. There comes a time to let go of toxic relationships that do not support your new growth. This includes letting go of dysfunctional family members and "friends." This includes avoiding the flying monkeys recruited by the narcissist to be his willing tools. This includes refusing to spend one second of your precious life energy stressing over stupid triangulations the abuser manipulates and creates. Let it all go. You were not allowed to choose your family, your culture, your race, or your biological gender. You were born into those realities. You can choose to not allow relational dysfunction to become a toxic gift that keeps on infecting your life, growth, and happiness. You can choose to not associate with past narcissistic partners, friends, family members, and people still embroiled within the abusive, vampire lifestyle. You have the power to deflect and avoid the predators and willing victims still enmeshed within the abusive culture of narcissism. You can avoid and disconnect from people who allow their personally chosen vampire *to ruin their lives, rule their decisions* and wreck their happiness. Dysfunctional people who will always choose misery over happiness are not healthy. They are not being honest or accountable with themselves. They are not ready to make change. It is perfectly healthy to avoid people who choose to live with a toxic, hyper competitive, monster. It is wise and in your own rational self-interest to avoid an abuser who is dedicated to always making someone else wrong and themselves always right. Dysfunctional people who defend and justify their abuser no matter the damming evidence or circumstances have agreed to be prey. Remember that the narcissist's ego and position are always connected. If his position falls, his enormous yet fragile ego will fall with his position. The narcissist will never allow this to happen. The vampire will go to any means needed to keep his position upright. The abuser gives no thought as to how illogical, harmful, or cruel his methods may be. The creature does not care how these methods affect others. Your goal is to find new role models and new friends that you can learn from. A role model is someone you choose to emulate so **choose wisely**. *Future Change will always happen because of your present moment choices, negative, positive, or indifferent.*

You are who you choose to become.

Here are my answers to the above questions:

1. **Who am I?** I am a being-becoming. I am a child of the universe and I am learning and growing always.

2. **What is my purpose?** My purpose is to serve and help others realize the truth of who they are and to help them know the truth of their being. To do this I must continue to learn and grow, to share as much as I can with my fellow Earthtribe brothers and sisters.

3. **What is the meaning of life?** The meaning of life is to learn the lessons of life with humility, grace and poise. *(I am still working hard on this.)*

4. **Is there life after death?** Nothing our Universe/ Source creates ever goes away as it only changes form. When a bonfire is lit the logs do not vanish, they change from a solid into a gas. They release

the energy that the sun gave to the tree. For me the spiritual principal "as above, so below" holds true. I come from an amazing, un-namable, Source. I am the collected debris from stars and universal expansion having a current physical experience. I am a stardust water being. Thus, when my body has served its Source driven purpose, transformation will occur. A new creation will come forth eventually. Source energy will continue. New lessons will manifest. My lessons will continue until learned. Then more lessons will follow.

5. **What does freedom mean to you?** *(I don't mean just escaping the vampire; I mean living as a free person.)*

Freedom is contained within the sure knowledge that we are never separate from our true Source. We cannot be separate from our Source for we are all the Source we are created from. We are divine beings for we are created from a Divine Source. Duality and separation from Source is an illusion. It is the grand illusion for it has kept us divided for centuries. Recognizing that we and our Source are one frees us from the two-camp continuum of "them" and "us." It releases us from hatred, racism, intolerance, and the toxic idea of lack and limitation. It frees us from the abuser spawned illusion that we must take from others because there is not enough to go around. When you know with certainty that you are the child of an unlimited Source that creates unlimited multi-verses, you find true freedom. When you finally realize who you really are you know with certainty that you have all you ever need. Furthermore, you are led to a life of service to others, for in serving others you serve Source (this cannot be otherwise) and thus align yourself with Source. This is true freedom. This is the only true freedom, for all else is an illusion that eventually enslaves.

"For you created my innermost being;

You knit me together in my mother's womb.

I praise you because I am fearfully and wonderfully made;

Your works are wonderful,

I know that full well.

My frame was not hidden from you,

When I was made in that secret place.

When I was woven together in the depths of the Earth,

Your eyes saw my unformed body.

All the days ordained for me

Were written in your book

Before one of them came to be me."

Psalm 139:13-16. The King James Bible.

Chapter Two suggestion: Research positive, successful people and pick one as an "imaginary" role model and mentor. After you have learned all you can about them, imagine they are giving you advice and life coaching. What would they say to you? What would they focus on? Write two pages of the advice and coaching they would give you and be specific about the challenges in your life they would address with you. Consider your own readiness to change. Think about personal accountability. How would your role model address accountability with you? You can pick anyone you want, living or dead, from Lincoln to Gandhi. If it is unsafe to write, then forgo writing until it is safe to do so and just contemplate as best you can. Use online forums safely and anonymously if needed.

This exercise is important for a very good reason. You are beginning to flex your mind like you flex your muscles. You are developing your **freedom of choice muscle**. You choose this role model, you choose these core values, and you make it all work. It is always your **response-ability** (*ability to respond*) that impacts your life for better or worse. You must find out what works for you. No one else can do that for you. You are unique, your challenges are unique to your situation, and no one else is going to figure it out better than you. A truly free life is a series of constant and changing situations that call for **choices and accountability**. A self-actualized, life consists of a series of constant and ongoing free will decisions. It is not in your rational self-interest to allow former associates and dangerous partners, or hurtful family relationships, to make or dictate those decisions for you.

CHOOSE WISELY

If you have expectations that a program or a person can make your decisions for you, you are doomed to failure. You are trying to avoid the responsibility and possibly the difficulty involved in choosing for yourself. You are expecting others to make your survival decisions. This is always a bad idea for it makes you weaker never stronger.

A role model is someone you admire for their habits, core values, and ethics. Role models can become a road map to a better life. By emulating their habits you will make some progress. However you must understand that you will most likely not duplicate everything about them. Their actions, and their lifestyle is always a result of their choices. It is your **responsibility** to find that job, school, training, therapy, relationship, or program that will work best for you and your unique situation. *Then you must work at it. Change will always happen because of choices. You are who you choose to become. Einstein's definition of insanity was to do the same thing over and over expecting a different result.*

"It is not the strongest of the species that survive,

Nor the most intelligent,

But the one most responsive to change."

- Charles Darwin

Chapter 2 Affirmations: *I love myself for I am love, and in so doing I share love with all around me who deserve my love.*

I enjoy finding healthy choices in my daily life.

I choose my friends wisely.

I like to engage with people who foster my healthy, self-growth.

I deserve freedom.

I recommend that you speak your chosen affirmation within your mind each night as you drift off to sleep. I also think you should say your affirmation to yourself for a few moments as you are waking up and preparing for your day. As you go through your day, bring your focus internally to your affirmation from time to time throughout the day. If you experience negative thoughts strive to overwhelm them with your affirmations. As you go through the chapters use the affirmations daily and feel free to mix them up throughout the week, however I recommend that you focus upon only one each day.

Remember: If you have become engulfed by the narcissistic games and negative thinking errors, you cannot expect to use an affirmation for only a minute or two each day and expect a quick result. Every negative and self-limiting utterance and verbal/physical violence behavior you accept from your narcissist is an affirmation all its own. IF YOU CHOOSE TO ACCEPT IT. For your affirmations to be successful you must be willing to use them every day and use them a lot! Affirmations can really help you notice self-limiting thoughts and beliefs because you will use them each time a negative thought comes up. Your awareness of your own internal dialogue will be raised. With raised awareness you will begin replacing the negative thoughts, insults, assertions, and dangerous beliefs of the vampire with positive, life affirming thoughts just for you. This will take some work on your part, but eventually it will become enjoyable work. Remember, your chosen affirmation should be the last thing you say to yourself as you are falling asleep and the first thought on your mind when you wake up each morning. This exercise helps you gain control over your thoughts. It helps you become stronger and more resistant to unhealthy people, places, and things. It helps you choose your own programming rather than just passively allowing programming by others. Positive affirmations can give your overworked hypothalamus a much-needed break. Your body will appreciate some time away from stress hormones.

You are not your past. You are not the reality the vampire defines for you. You are not what the abuser decides to label you. You are not your emotions. You are what you accept you are. You are powerful, and you can decide to live your life authentically. If you accept the vampire's decisions, you will become the out picturing of those decisions. The vampire only becomes stronger when you decide to feed it. You are strong enough to starve this parasite out of your life. You must learn to starve the creature for your own health and wellbeing. If you starve the narcopath by refusing to play toxic communication games, the chaos minion will discard you eventually. Are you afraid of being discarded? Even by a dysfunctional, dangerous, life draining idiot? Only you know this answer, and if you answer yes to this question then you have some personal growth work to begin right away. If you answered no to this question, then why are you still with the vampire or still interacting with him? Break off or limit contact immediately.

Sometimes we learn to accept chaos and dysfunction because it became our comfort zone when growing up. Babies are not born with word-connected thought. They learn it gradually from the "giants" that surround them. The giants either make the baby feel better or they do not. Sometimes they fall somewhere in the middle by hurting, helping, and being indifferent. The baby learns what the baby is taught. The baby learns that giants can be trusted or not trusted, or sometimes both trusted and not trusted. What kind of baby were you? What is your comfort zone? Only you can answer this question. Your narcissist already knows the answer even if he cannot articulate the answer. The narcissist knows exactly what kind of victims to zero in upon. He can detect empathy, compassion, and co-dependency like a shark can detect one-part blood in a million parts water. The narcissist is always hunting for new supply. The narcissistic relationship always has an expiration date. The infectious level of dysfunctional communication guarantees an unhappy ending. As I have pointed out previously, the abuser always damages his tools.

"You must discard that old, outdated, fear driven survival skill of denial left over from your life placating and feeding a toxic vampire. You must replace that skill with a new, free world survival skill, **Self-Honesty**."

Chapter 3

Guilt, Anger, Regret.

GUILT.

You sub-consciously choose to feel guilt.

Your narcissist knows this instinctively. He uses it against you. Narcissists love to manipulate people with guilt. Guilt fits in perfectly as a support mechanism for destructive, narcissistic victimhood. Guilt fits so well with victimhood that both covert and overt narcissists use guilt as a tool for manipulation. Guilt is not something a vampire is burdened with however. To feel guilt, you must first possess empathy and compassion. Abusers possess neither. Guilt trips work when you do not understand your own emotions. You think you have no control over your emotions. You think your emotions are "you." That is not correct. The narcissist uses emotions as well as compassion and empathy (Yours) to control, manipulate, and drain his victims. He is an energy leech and his energy needs are instinctively driven and obtained. His ability to appeal to you emotionally keeps him connected. He will pathologically discard you eventually with relative ease. This is because he has developed no actual emotional attachment to you. He is incapable of actual love. Love requires compassion and empathy. He is an expert at gaining your emotional attachment while he stays disconnected emotionally. The dangerous creature fakes/mimics emotion on command when it serves a purpose. The vampire only reflects back to you your own humanity, for it possesses no authentic humanity. The narcopath is both tragedy, and predator in one. The vampire is the tragic predator, and as such, it is very dangerous. A vampire becomes a vampire because of a bite, however this makes the creature no less dangerous to you personally. A monster created by nature or nurture is still a monster. Do not allow the vampires dangerous ability to mimic emotion to exert control over your life.

When you live in guilt you live in the past, bound to the past by ancient choices you made. Decisions you made that had results. Old realities that played out years ago. You cannot change those decisions you made in the past. Nor can you change the results of those past decisions. You have grown and learned new information, there is no doubt about this fact. Life has taught you many things that you may not yet realize. Do not allow your past choices to define you in the present moment. Don't allow memories of those past choices to affect your hypothalamus today. Those past choices and decisions taught you your life lessons. They have influenced your life and your "now" but you don't have to stay bound up in the past. You do not have to allow the past to dictate your present or your future. You may think you are trapped and that life will never change. You may feel helpless and unable to make change. You may feel hopeless and believe that hopelessness will stay as a constant reality within your life. If you feel hopelessly trapped, you just do not realize your own power. You are a change maker. Accept this reality. By making new choices today you will create a new future. This cannot be avoided. You most likely would not make the same choices today that you made years in the past if faced with identical circumstances. Your choices today will influence your life in the future. This is a powerful tool that you possess. Your power and ability to choose shapes your future. It influences your loved one's future also. The vampire loves to use guilt as a control tool. Do not allow this clumsy attempt at manipulation. The past is dead, and the future has yet to be born.

Guilt is a secondary emotion.

You remember your past decision, the result of that decision, and you suddenly feel guilt. The thoughts of your past came first, along with other emotions attached to them. It was then that guilt showed up. Guilt is really a useless emotion at this stage of your life. No one has the power to change the past. It is just not possible, so it makes no sense to dwell in the past. It makes no logical sense to beat yourself up over decisions made in the past. Your new decisions today are the most important ones for you right now. Narcissists use guilt to manipulate their supply source. By keeping you focused on the dead past they keep you from living within the live present. Do not allow your past choices to be used within the present moment to manipulate you. *Guilt does nothing to foster your new growth.*

Many people are under the impression that narcissists are just misunderstood, perpetual children. They think you "should have known better." They may view your questioning of the old, unhealthy relationship dynamic negatively. Sometimes they may perceive the processing of your past and present challenges as "victimhood." Your new growth, and emerging self-worth is not "victimhood." It is new growth, new direction, and new focus. You are creating a new way of being in the world. Do not have any expectation of understanding about your situation from people who have never experienced narcissistic abuse. If they have never been abused by either a romantic partner, spouse, or parent just expect that they will not be able to relate to your experience. Do not expect a therapist to automatically understand you. Therapists are just people and they have their own challenges. I believe that most of them do their best. Be ready for mental health professionals to see the minion of chaos as a victim. In doing so they may unintentionally minimize your challenges. Do not allow yourself to fall into resentment about their perceptions. Do not fall into the guilt trap due to anyone else's judgments of *your* past. Do not allow their understanding of the narcissistic relationship dynamic to define your needs. Their reality is not yours and your reality is not theirs. They did not make your choices. Your life lessons belong to you. Do not allow guilt from a past you cannot change to influence your choices today. No one has the power to make you feel anything. *You possess the power to choose how you feel; you just don't realize this fact at this moment in time.* You have experienced some life lessons due to unwise or uninformed choices. The healthiest decision now is to accept the lessons learned and resolve to make healthy choices. This is done within the only place you can choose to do so: **the present moment**. You only have the present moment, moment to moment, in which to make healthy change and decisions. You can rarely change people's beliefs. Don't bother trying. You cannot change the past and you are not yet in the future. You have only this present moment. *Use this moment well.*

Once you realize and accept the true power you have over your emotions and thoughts you will experience a great internal freedom. If you allow yourself to succumb to the secondary emotion of guilt you are on the road to hopelessness. You are on the road back to one narcissistic relationship after another. You are still mentally imprisoned by the vampire dynamic and you will compulsively seek it out again. Chaos has become your comfort zone. The narcissistic dynamic may feel familiar to you. You may understand how to survive in chaos, but this understanding is not due to psychologically healthy reasons. You are still trapped in the past. You are still experiencing your old, outdated past choices and not accepting the new lessons learned here within the present moment.

The apostle Paul was once named Saul. Saul was a mass murderer and a violent man. Had he allowed guilt and his unchangeable past to define him and thus rule his present moment choices he would never have made it off the road to Damascus. *He would never have transformed and thus allowed the truth of his Divine Source and Being-Becoming to manifest and become Paul.* Had he chosen to succumb to guilt from past life choices that no longer represented his new growth and direction, he would have remained trapped within darkness. Instead of learning from past errors in thinking and perception which gave him great spiritual insight, he never would have written anything positive. He would never have become an apostle of Jesus. His writing inspires people today towards positive life choices. His writing is a direct result of his embracing a new way of being in the world. He created a completely new life, and with this life came new choices and new opportunities. *Paul became a new man due to his choices.* He could no longer be separate from the truth of his being. He left "Saul" behind because his old way of life was invalidated by the demands of new growth required for a *Being-Becoming.* He had free will and he used it. If "Saul" can choose to listen to Source and leave behind an old life of mass murder and hatred, you can also choose a new life. Paul was ready for a new way of being in the world and radical change became the truth of his being. Saul gained insight, and this manifested by out-picturing his Divine Source through his new self as "Paul." You too can you leave your past behind. Such is the transformative power of readiness to change. Use your free will and choose wisely. You can become an entirely new man or woman. You can outgrow the narcissistic, abusive relationship. You can invalidate the old, outdated narcissistic relationship by embracing powerful new growth. Others have done exactly this and so can you.

You are not your past.

Your past is only an ancient reflection of old choices invalidated by new growth within the present moment. Know this without a doubt. You are neither your past nor your past decisions. You are much more than just the sum total of old situations. Your life lessons have been gifts of hard won knowledge. If you have been paying attention these gifts have added to your ability to make healthy choices. Your *current vampire is a consequence for unwise decisions. However the vampire is also a powerful learning experience.* Some choices may have been made for you by other people. Possibly judges, lawyers, therapists, social service agencies, juries, family members, parents, and police officers were involved in your life. Some choices were made by the narcissistic monster you allowed into your life and these choices affected you. Your life may have been managed by others in the past. Control may have been taken from you for a while due to parents who were minions of chaos. You had no choice in who your parents were. Eventually however, we all become wise enough to change the course of our lives. Later on in life perhaps you made some choices that allowed control to be taken from you. Your relationships with your family and loved ones suffered because of the narcissistic relationship process. This was a direct result of old choices you once made within a long ago, currently invalidated past. You cannot change past decisions within the present moment. You can only change (and make) present moment choices. You suffered abuse as you went through life with a vampire. You endured the pain along with its co-occurring life lessons. The silver lining in this cloud is that you have completed the lessons. Now you can recognize that you have gained some co-occurring knowledge. You can move on.

You cannot change the past or how some past choices and decisions have affected you and those you love. There is only one healthy path open to you right now, within this present moment: *Change the way you live in the present by making healthy new choices. All your healthy choices right now are creating a positive future yet unknown to you.* The vampire has drank its fill of your energy for long enough. Your personal growth and awareness has balanced the scales. Life has banged its sacred gavel. *It's time to move on. You have survived the vampire, now survive its negative conditioning. See through its logical fallacies and thinking errors. Do not allow the past to define you now. Choose to thrive, not just survive.*

You are who you choose to become.

You are not your past choices.

ANGER.

Anger is another useless and always secondary emotion. You are not your anger and you sub-consciously **choose** to become angry. You allow anger to manifest. Anger is a tool of the abuser. Toxic anger from the abuser directed at you can infect you. Anger has ruined lives. Anger has destroyed people. Anger has sent more people into prison than all other emotions combined. If you are in a toxic, narcissistic dynamic right now, anger can only help feed the vampire. Un-managed anger can crush your plans, ruin your life, and possibly eliminate your freedom **forever**. *Anger can absolutely destroy your life and alter your life path.*

You are not your anger.

You choose to be angry.

An exercise in forgiveness, releasing the Debt:

Almost all words have multiple definitions. One of the definitions of forgiveness is to "let go of the debt." Many people have a hard time with forgiveness, especially if it involves forgiving someone who abused or neglected them. In the case of childhood abuse, many survivors carry around deep seated resentment, anger, and a sense of having something stolen from them. They feel violated. They carry the underlying feeling that the abuser owes them something, (a childhood for example.) This resentment is also common as one emerges from narcissistic abuse into full realization of the actual relationship dynamic.

If someone owed you fifty thousand dollars you would want to be compensated. If you hunted them for years, and finally found them in a gutter, wearing rags, barefoot and homeless, could you collect that fifty thousand? No. If you feel that your parents owed you a childhood and you never experienced a childhood; can you collect that childhood today? No. Do you think the narcissist "owes" you a healthy relationship? Do you think he can be "healed?" Do you think your efforts can "fix" him? He is just as incapable of giving you a healthy relationship as the guy sleeping in the gutter, barefoot and homeless could ever give you fifty thousand dollars. *Letting go of the debt can be the healthiest "selfish" thing you can do.* Carrying around a sense of loss, resentment, anger, even hatred, only hurts your health and future relationships with people. It saps your vital energy and lowers your ability to live life to its fullest. Carrying around the toxic weight of anger and its co-occurring resentment are not in your own rational self-interest. It can only foment toxicity. It wrecks your present moment peace.

Write out your answers to the following questions (if it is safe to do so.) Use other sheets of paper if needed.

As you write your answers remember:

Choices are everywhere, and choices impact the future as well as the present. Allowing your anger, resentment, and guilt to rule your choices will lead only to despair. You will be allowing past narcissistic manipulation and conditioning to dictate your interaction with the world. You will be doing what you think you want to do. You will actually be doing what an energy draining predator trained you to do. You will think you are in control when in fact you have no control. You will lose the ultimate war for your personal autonomy and freedom if you allow anger, resentment, and guilt to dictate your choices. Even when you are free of the narcissistic relationship you will remain a victim and prisoner of the vampire. You will think like a victim and act like a victim. You will eventually return to the place where victims live out their lives. You will return to another vampire. All of it will reflect your choices.

Has something been taken you cannot ever recover? Describe what you lost.

How much time per day do you think about your loss? Does this help or change anything?

If you could go back in time and change things, what would you change?

How would you be different?

How would you be the same?

What baggage are you carrying every day over this debt?

How will you feel without this baggage weighing on your mind?

Read everything you have written out loud or quietly, burn this worksheet (if possible) and release the debt, lighten your load. Repeat as needed.

Your past is only an ancient reflection of old choices invalidated by new growth in the present moment.

The Haiku Exercise

Japanese Haiku is a form of Japanese poetry. A traditional form of Japanese Haiku consists of a three-line poem. The first line has only five syllables, the second line seven syllables, and the third line five syllables. Here is one of my Haikus as an example:

> *One moon together*
>
> *Forever in time it stays*
>
> *Constant as one love*

The Samurai wrote haiku to strengthen, balance, and calm their minds. They believed that the constraints of the syllabic form created a strength of mind that gave the poet more creative ability. Your assignment is to use the haiku form to encapsulate an anger or conflict trigger. Once that is done you will use the same form to encapsulate a peaceful solution. Finally, you will create a haiku that conveys a peaceful concept, idea, or scene. The scene can be from nature, the ocean, a garden, weather, or any peaceful image you can imagine. When you are done you will have a nine-line haiku/poem. Here is my poem as an example:

Your rage shakes my house

And my rage, uncaged, begins

Where can I find peace?

I know your resin

Exists not in my forest

Peace is within me

My ocean glistens

My moonlight universal

My sky eternal

The Haiku exercise is an exercise that will, over time, strengthen your contemplation and focus. Both are useful and essential skills in managing anger and conflict. If you are currently in an unhealthy, abusive relationship you may have to schedule time away from the vampire. Your time is best spent quietly creating your individual haikus. It will not be useful to attempt including the vampire in this exercise because the energy leech is not capable of honesty. The creature will only attempt to control the outcome. There will be no talking during this exercise, just contemplation and creation. The vampire will only desire to manipulate and direct your behavior for his benefit. He will attempt manipulation via running his untruthful, virulent mouth. The vampire has no compassion, and this is a compassion-based exercise. Resist your empathic instinct to try and "heal" the creature by sharing your insights. This exercise is a waste of time when attempted by minions of chaos. Today is your day for self-compassion. You are worth it. Follow the silence rule as you create. Turn off the phone, computer, and TV. Eliminate distractions do this exercise alone if possible. All healthy solutions require some contemplation beforehand. This exercise is one I encourage you to use throughout your life. Use it both before and and after being in a relationship with an abusive, narcopathic, assclown. The contemplation of healthy solutions requires some dedicated practice.

The Resentment exercises.

The resentment exercise is concerned with helping individuals begin the steps to forgiveness. Most people who are chronically angry give away too much of their own personal power to the abusive people in their lives. Many people give away their power to life situations they resent. They allow the vampire to "rent space in their mind." They allow this when they could be using that precious space to focus upon their own happiness. Instead of focusing on the vampire's daily drama they could be focusing on their own creative projects, their dreams, and the people close to them. They could be using their mind to become inspired by life.

The path to forgiveness needs three important steps:

1. Acknowledge your true feelings about the relational situation with your narcissist/abuser that causes your resentment.

2. Recognize the personal cost of your energy leech. Be honest about how much this unwholesome relationship and its co-occurring resentment hurts and drains you. Consider the energy you expend on this resentment every day.

3. Focus on the benefits of letting the anger and its co-occurring resentment go. Sometimes long-term anger is frightening to let go of. Especially if it has been your personal companion for so long that life may be scary without it at your side. If anger makes you feel strong or powerful, you might feel weak or defenseless without it anymore. The opposite is actually true. The more anger energy you use in long term resentment, the less energy and focus you have available for issues that need your awareness and attention. Anger is not a healthy fuel. Anger consumes its vehicle for expression (you.) Narcissistic vampires love to feed upon their supply. They drain their victims of time, energy, and happiness daily. They will eagerly consume negative and positive emotional

energy. Please don't feed the vampire. Abusers will consume your anger as fuel. That is why they have so much pestilence available. They fill up on anger every chance they get.

You are not your anger.

Your past is only an ancient reflection of old choices invalidated by new growth in the present moment.

You are not your past.

The exercise: Be honest and *address the three steps to forgiveness in writing and do so quietly.* Once you are finished with the questions inherent within the three steps, take some time for yourself. Honestly consider how toxic resentment and anger towards your narcissist affects your interactions with other people. What personal goals in your life has the energy leech compromised? Are you taking the classes you want to take? Do you go to a gym? Do you have hobbies? Do you have friends? Do you have a career? Do you walk on eggshells around your narcissist? What do you sacrifice for this relationship with the vampire? When you are doing this exercise just remember to turn off your phone, computer, and TV. Do the exercise in a quiet place where you will remain undisturbed. *Remember, the more resentment and its co-occurring anger you carry around with you each day, the less response-ability to have for life lessons, opportunities, and challenges.* Unresolved anger and resentment will stifle your creativity, your communication, and your relationships. Un-managed anger can be a catalyst for unhealthy interactions within society. The vampire does not deserve your inner light, effort, nor your attention. The creature does not give anything but chaos. The energy leech can only drain you.

You are not your anger. You are not your past. You are not your resentment.

Anger is not a healthy fuel, as anger only consumes its vehicle for expression (you.)

The Vampire starvation exercise.

The path to physical violence and confrontation has three predictable stages recognized by researchers. The verbal phase, the posturing phase, and the physical phase. The verbal and posturing phases are almost always co-occurring. They involve tone of voice, body language, facial expressions and blended micro-expressions. Researchers agree that over 90% of all aggression begins and ends in the verbal and posturing phases of conflict. This exercise will help you understand the power that verbal and non-verbal communication wield in conflict resolution and anger management.

Choices are everywhere, and choices impact the future as well as the present.

Your choices in the heat of an unthoughtful moment can be the catalyst that propels you back into the vampire's world and keeps you there. If you allow your secondary emotions to control your thoughts and those thoughts control your actions, you will be just another energy source for a narcissist. Someone else's tone of voice, opinion, or body language belongs to them alone. It is their reality within their present moment. Don't make it your reality. Stop playing the narcissists game. The vampire only wants to control you, feed on your energy, drain you, and eventually discard you. *Your response is all yours, always. You cannot control what others do and say but you have total control over what you do and say.*

The exercise:

This one will be tough. Practice listening to your narcissist. You can also do this exercise at work or within family gatherings. You can do it anywhere Narcopaths exist. This is a useful exercise that will help you raise awareness if you have narcissists in your life. Listen without any intention of arguing with them. Just detach and pay close attention. I know this will be a difficult task. Perhaps you can practice when they are on the phone or talking to another family member or friend. Find an opportunity. Observe their verbal and posturing manipulation efforts as if you are detached from your body. Identify their thinking errors and logical fallacies. If the narcissist is speaking directly with you be vigilant but relaxed. Monitor your tone of voice so that the narcissist does not escalate to unsafe levels of verbal conflict. Practice using your tone of voice and body language to direct the narcissist away from the physical phase. This phase is almost always associated with direct violence. Once the physical phase is reached the conflict can become dangerous and possibly life threatening.

Pay attention as to how the narcissist manipulates the conversation into a contest. Watch and listen for the obvious verbal and posturing phases. Pay close attention to ways the vampire uses inherent logical fallacies and thinking errors to control and regulate communication. Listen for closed ended questions and arrogant, "know it all" statements. Listen for any statement containing an assumed premise. Calmly observe how the narcissist desperately works hard to manipulate the flow and direction of the conversation. Just listen and observe how the narcissist transforms the conversation into a contest that they always win. It is very important for you to recognize and observe how their "communication" is conflict driven. Look at the way they employ aggression, both overt aggression and passive aggression. Listen for put downs and insults both direct and indirect. Do this exercise so you can learn to recognize these toxic communication patterns within other people you encounter in life. Do not confront or attack the vampire's position. Use your own communication skills both verbal, and body language to become almost un-noticeable. Observe ways to de-escalate the situation. Practice your "I statements," facial expressions, and tone of voice. Learn to communicate in such a way as to deflect and re-direct the narcissistic, abusive idiot. Calm down the situation. An example of an "I statement" is: "I hear what you are saying," or "I want to understand." Another one is "I feel minimized when you insult my feelings." Prepare for new overt and covert insults and passive-aggressive behaviors to surface during the exercise. Afterwards, away from the manipulative vampire, process what you observed and learned. Remember, you don't want to feed him with negative or positive energy, you just want to learn his patterns.

I have met with many people struggling with narcissistic abuse, discard, and abandonment issues. Sometimes they carry around anger, resentment, fear, hatred, longing, regret, and even rage against the narcissist who abused them. They will claim to HATE not only the narcissist, but the counselors, therapists, judges, and other people who became involved in the narcissistic/abusive relationship. They sometimes hold deep resentment for the police (who seem to almost always allow the narcissist to get away with his manipulations,) as well as family members, former friends, etc. They claim to hate the mental health system, the justice system, and even themselves sometimes. They commonly have an internal dialog that blames themselves for their abusive situation. Hate, anger, and resentment have become a regular part of their internal reality. Sometimes they report that they still "miss" their narcissist. This is all very unhealthy. This is also championship level denial.

Anger is a secondary emotion always. You choose to be angry. Your response is all yours, always. You cannot control what others do and say but you have total control over what you do and say.

The Narcissist is an instinct and ego driven vampire. The narcissist is always thirsty for energy. A narcissist simply cannot hang out a **NO VACANCY** sign because he is driven by an aggressive and pathological instinct to feed. Once you became an adult it was you and only you who made the conscious and unconscious choices to land yourself in front of a minion of chaos. You arrived within the vampire's den due to the choices you made on a certain day and time. Before you showed up they never knew of your existence. They will not think about you after they discard and destroy you. They will enjoy feeding on your energy and they will enjoy your pain. They will discard you when they have no more use for you. They will simply monkey branch to their next willing source of supply once they have located it. If they remember you at all, they will remember the pain they caused you and smile. The silver lining in this temporary cloud is that you also have the power to consciously choose to starve the vampire out of your life.

"Anger is not a healthy fuel, as anger only consumes its vehicle for expression."

Consider the following questions:

Why would you continue to dwell upon the toxic vampire?

What purpose does it serve?

How does holding on to resentment fuel your new growth?

How does anger help you find true purpose in life?

You choose to be angry, you choose to seek peace. You can choose to let go of anger.

Staying angry at your narcissist is a waste of your precious energy, time, and resources. It is also a source of fuel for the narcissist. Staying angry at yourself for the situation is also an equally useless pastime. You are just wasting your precious and finite life energy. You are losing time and resources that can be better spent on good times with friends and loved ones. Don't squander energy, time, and resources that you can use to better your life. Use your life energy to fund you own creative projects, act in your own rational self-interest, and grow in healthier directions. Throughout all this *time* you have had choices. Many more choices are in store for you. The choices will never stop. *Lessons will continue until learned.*

If you alter your attitude about life, you will change how you view your life, your life will change.

REGRET.

Regret is another secondary emotion and it is useless. The past is truly dead and over with. You cannot change the past any more than you can time travel. Regret is akin to giving medicine to a corpse and expecting it to work. Regret only hurts your present moment awareness. The present moment in time is the only moment you can now make choices within. The future has not happened, the past has already happened. Regret has no use within your present moment. Malignant regret cannot help you grow. Regret is only dwelling on past choices that fed the vampire. Consider your lessons learned, let go of regret and move into the light of understanding.

Regret is a time bandit. Time is precious, don't waste a second of it.

You simply do not possess the power to change anything already done and over with. You can make amends, you can set healthy boundaries, you can see past choices as life lessons and learn from those past choices. You can go grey rock or no contact and starve your Narcopath. You can acknowledge that there are always multiple choices available. You can recognize that in the past you did not see all the choices you had *due to choices made with emotion rather than reason*. You can accept that you did not see all the positive possibilities available to you. You can see the patterns of the vampire and learn from them. You can accept responsibility for past choices and learn from those choices, but you cannot change past choices. You can only make and change present choices.

Regret is optional, never mandatory.

The words you spoke or did not speak, the actions you took or avoided, the other available choices you did not see or consider, these things are over with. They are done. They are lost to time and not present within the now. *They exist only in your mind. Do not let these past situations influence your present choices by blinding you to present positive possibilities.* You are not your past; you are much more than that. Look for other choices that are available within the present moment. Your choices today will influence your tomorrow. You can create a tomorrow free of the abuser.

The only action you can take in the present moment is to accept the past and its lessons, learn from those lessons, and move on. Any other action allows the past to rule your present moment and all you have is your present moment. Regret is a time bandit. Don't allow regret to rob you of your present moment in time.

Regret is a secondary emotion, thus you and only you choose regret. You choose to dwell in regret, to lose the present moment, to stay in regret. You choose to make decisions and choices from regret. Choose instead to stay within the present moment always.

Thought is powerful. Everything begins with a thought. My laptop, my cell phone, my truck, all started with thought. Someone first visualized their creation and then brought the vision into being. All empirical creation begins with with thought, then it is conceptualized on paper or upon a computer, then it is created. You can observe this process with a three-dimensional printer. *Thought is beautiful.* You are a thinking being and you cannot help it. Thought begins everything and thought began your path to narcissistic abuse. Thought is the only way to a new path. Thought can also lead you away from future narcissistic abuse. You must allow it and direct it to do so. No one else can do this for you.

Thought can help you stay free from a vampire.

You will encounter people on your path in life. Some will be encouraging of your new growth, some will only want to bring up your past. Some people will have strong opinions, some will be neutral. A narcissist will reflect towards you what you seem to desire. This is done in a toxic, pathological effort to find a lever to use for the extraction of your energy. Your empathy is seen as a weakness to them. Something they can take advantage of for later feeding. A common (Stalking) tactic of narcissists is to mine your social media for information they can use later. Expect the narcissistic vampire to use shaming language for manipulation purposes. Your phone is not safe from them either. You cannot control other people's thoughts and actions. Since their words and actions spring from their thoughts and you are not a mind reader, you will not see their actions coming nor anticipate their words. When you meet people who judge you by the past or attempt to use your past to manipulate you, recognize the game. Just know that they are living in the past. Refuse to argue with them. Don't try to "convince" them of anything. It is a waste of your precious time. They are speaking from their beliefs, experiences, and ego. The ego centered person just wants to make everyone wrong and themselves right, always. They are trying to bring up your past to make you "wrong" within the present moment. Whenever your past is brought up in your present moment, judgement is the goal. Do not accept this dynamic. *You are not your past.*

When you become defensive or argue with a narcissist/abuser you are just playing ego games. You are doubting yourself and your present moment choices. You are giving away your personal power by accepting their manipulations, negativity, and thinking errors. You are still presently living with toxic judgements and accepting these judgements as valid. You are dwelling in the past right alongside them. You are losing time in the present moment and your energy is focused upon feeding the vampires infectious, unfillable ego. You are justifying your own ego and defending a dead past rather than your new growth. The abuser has succeeded in diverting you from your new path. You are squandering your precious energy upon the past. A past that cannot be changed. This is all just an exercise in futility, as it is just a feeding mechanism for the vampire. Do not buy into this narcissistic false construct. Once you have no value or respect for their opinion you will have no use for their opinion. You are on your way to freedom. You are walking into the light of personal autonomy. The minions of chaos hate the light of freedom.

If you want to change other people's opinions, show them rather than tell them. To be an example requires choice always.

Do not allow other people's value judgments based upon their own ego constructs to influence your self-worth. Flawed beliefs about your past choices should have no power to control your present decisions. Refuse to allow the narcissists misrepresentations of your life to influence your precious and finite present moments. You are not your emotions nor your past. Ignore the flying monkeys and avoid triangulation as best you can. Grey rock or no contact will eliminate them eventually. These people, places, and things only help feed the narcissist. Begin using thought to create positive, life affirming choices that result in a positive, present moment life. This will take some sincere effort on your part to not engage with negative people. Just know that every time you engage a person who is determined to bring up the past, *you are not in the present*. Instead, you are allowing them to make you live within the past. Use "I" statements and positive affirmations such as; *"I like to live in the present, not the past." "I make better choices now." "I have learned from my past and have accepted the lessons."* Then get away from the negative person as fast as you can do so. Negative thinking takes a toll on you. Guilt, anger, and regret depend upon the past to keep you trapped. That's why the vampire uses them so pathologically against you. The emotions triggered by guilt, anger, and regret can block you from seeing positive possibilities and choices. These secondary emotions only help and enable the narcissist to feed upon your energy. You are not your past, the past is dead, and the future is not yet here. Live right now. Make your present moment the place where positive choices are made. Take back your life from the abuser.

Your response is all yours, always. You cannot control what others do and say but you have total control over

what you do and say within each precious moment in time.

"Do not allow other people's value judgments based upon their own ego constructs about your past choices to influence your precious present moments. You are not your emotions nor your past. Begin using thought to create positive, life affirming choices that result in a positive, present moment life."

Chapter Three Affirmations: *I affirm with love and acceptance that I cannot be separate from that which created me.*

I am worthy of joy.

I love life.

I enjoy learning.

I accept only that which fosters my new growth.

I do not allow anyone to feed on my precious energy.

Chapter 4

Humanize Yourself

The narcissistic abuse process may cause you to become numb in some areas of your consciousness. This process affects how you see yourself and how you perceive the world around you. It attacks your basic humanity. It is not uncommon to feel imprisoned. You will soon forget the simple things you used to enjoy as a vampire-free person. You may reminisce sometimes about driving your car on an unplanned road trip, but you know deep inside that this will never happen. As long as you stay with the vampire your basic autonomy will be crushed. You may dream of going to a restaurant that you picked out, but you will not remember the last time you ever decided on a dining establishment. Abusers have a way of making all the decisions and dictating the terms of the relationship. Over time, the mind-numbing monotony and *freedom from choice* inherent within a relationship with a parasite will poison you. The day to day unwholesome routine of an abuse filled life will crush your spirit. Vampire inspired madness will divert any healthy instinct away from rational self-interest. Narcissistic driven drama will have influenced the way you think. After a few years of vampire driven life, you'll sadly accept the life you have co-created with the narcissistic monster. *You will be in effect eating garbage and calling it ice cream.* This un-healthy dynamic happened over time. Slowly you began to accept things as they were, dreaming about what they might become later. Living within an imaginary future that simply cannot manifest with an abuser in your life. You were dreaming of a bright future that could never grow from the darkness of your present relationship. A future unlikely to manifest due to the vampire draining your energy. Your current and past circumstances coupled with poor choices have created and sustained the present. What would have been perceived as a nightmare by a free-thinking person became your daily grind. You have become used to being used as a supply source for an unquenchable, drama driven monster. This energy leeching process was a gradual one so strive to be kind to yourself. Please remember that the narcissist can only mimic empathy and compassion. It cannot behave authentically with another human being because our humanity is based upon honest communication. The vampire is an infectious manipulator. As social creatures, how we relate to one another is important. Emotional authenticity is the foundation for true communication. *You became the narcissist's prisoner psychologically and thus you began to act like a prisoner socially.*

Seeing this process can begin growth in a new direction.

I am asking you to remember your childhood. Do not focus on what you didn't have or who was cruel to you.   Don't focus on your narcissistic family members, parents or siblings. *I want something different from you.* Were there things you loved to do? Were there things you wanted to do but you were not able to do them? If you could do them today, would you? When you played deeply, what were your innermost thoughts?   What did you daydream about?   What did you want to become? Who did you want to be? Did you have heroes? Who were they?   Why were they heroes to you? I am asking you to think deeply and fearlessly about these things. I want you to remember the songs of your spirit. *The dreams of childhood that whispered to your heart.*

Remember what you loved before you were a supply source for the vampire.

Can you remember a time when you could enjoy yourself without worrying about the monster's approval, drama, or toxic opinion? Over time, people involved in toxic or destructive relationships develop unhealthy thinking patterns. Pleasures once enjoyed without the narcissist in your life become forgotten pleasures. Over time the enmeshment into the narcissistic relationship becomes the focus of your life. Then the abusive process makes you a slave as it hijacks your brain. This unbalanced, toxic life becomes your new normal. Your brain is an expert at making connections. The more those connections are used the stronger they become. *You attract into your life what you think about.* The basic, simple pleasures are still there for you, however unnoticed they may have become. If you choose to seek those pleasures again, you will find them. You originally enjoyed those pleasures without a narcissistic monster draining you. *You also have the power to seek out new pleasures, to do the things you only dreamed about as a child. You have the power to create new connections. New life experiences become new connections. New connections become a new pathway.*

You have the power to choose. Choose wisely.

Throughout all this time you have had choices. Many more choices are in store for you. The choices will never stop. Lessons will continue until learned. I know a woman who took up surfing at forty-nine years old. She had been in a terrible and abusive relationship with a drama driven, control freak. The Narcopathic idiot she married dominated her life. After her divorce she was depressed, extremely angry, and lost. She became addicted to prescription pills and was for all intents and purposes a "legal" drug addict. A friend introduced her to surfing and she loves it and does well at it. This surprises many people at the beach where I surfed, and body boarded for years. Many people expressed self-limiting thoughts and beliefs about a person almost fifty years old beginning to surf. Especially a person with her challenges. She obtained counseling and began the journey of rediscovering pleasure without drug use. More importantly she began a journey towards rediscovering a life free of narcissistic abuse. She reported that her real healing came when she realized she did not need her narcissistic vampire at all. This was a direct result of her being no longer interested in his opinion or the opinions of his flying monkeys. His vile triangulations had no effect on her because she was too busy growing in new, healthy directions. She found out that she no longer needed to dull her consciousness in order to live her life. On the way back to herself she remembered many things she dreamed about doing. Dreams she was unable to even attempt due to her dysfunctional relationship. One of them was to play in the Pacific Ocean. When she was finally "done" with the vampire's drama and constant drain upon her life force she began to heal. She was no longer "bleeding" energy. While in the toxic relationship she had developed some self-limiting thoughts and beliefs about herself. These self-limiting thoughts became her very own toxic affirmations. When she had attempted surfing years ago, her future ex-husband/narcopath had openly mocked her efforts. Co-occurring dysfunctional family members had ridiculed her and sabotaged her attempts at playing in the beautiful Pacific Ocean. *Feeling trapped within a world of anger, domestic violence, and hopelessness she just gave up. Thus, she never put on a wetsuit or touched a board. She had allowed this to happen. Her surfing dream had never manifested.* She was trapped in the narcissist's web of deceit, gas-lighting, triangulation, dishonesty, and abuse. Pills and alcohol were her ways of "checking out." Numbing her feelings became her escape. The escape route became her new "normal." The minions of chaos were being well fed.

"You do not need permission from anyone to think, however you may need your own permission to think."

The ocean was five minutes from her house and most days she never even noticed it was there. She never listened to its call. She drove by two surf shops every day and never went inside either of them. *Her heart cried out for the ocean and she could not bring herself to listen. She chose instead to ignore its guidance and thus lost years upon the waves.* **Your choices within the present moment become your future.** She listened to her narcissist, accepted his toxic opinions and manipulations, and lived enmeshed within an abusive relationship. She chose to ignore her inner voice and did not realize she was ignoring it. She had to rediscover pleasure, she had to remember her long ago dream of one day being able to surf. The secret dreams of her spirit were always there, waiting for her to accept them. She had to **choose** to claim that dream and make it real. Despite being forty-nine years old, despite the violence of others and *their* self-limiting thoughts, beliefs, and judgments. She began to heal with a thought. One healthy thought strengthened other healthy thoughts. Despite the vampire and his toxic, pathological lifestyle, her thoughts became unstoppable. She began to move into the light of freedom. The opinion of the vampire became meaningless to her. The flying monkeys became powerless. The triangulations became dust in the wind.

On the way to freedom she found other things she loved to do also. Just for the sake of doing them. *Just because they were fun.* One day, on the beach she said to me "Dante, surfing is better than any drug!" Other people overhearing her comment scoffed and had judgmental looks upon their faces. They did not understand her reality and that is ok, why should we expect them to understand it? *Their judgments and self-limiting thoughts and beliefs simply did not matter within her present moment.* She had claimed her bliss, she had found her passion and she was in love with it. She had the wonder of a child about surfing and she was allowing no one to steal that wonder from her ever again. She body boarded and surfed with her sons and found a profound joy within this endeavor. This helped her heal from years of narcissistic abuse and helped her sons heal also. She had found and embraced the forgotten dreams of her spirit.

What you cannot currently do does not have to influence what you can currently accomplish.

She found healing. She found happiness. She was no longer dependent upon the opinions of other people. The narcissist and his constant gaslighting, his flying monkeys, his toxic demands, his twisted triangulations, had no more power over her life. She had found fun again, she surfed, and body boarded simply because it made her entire being sing. She had no expectations of others and no need to seek their approval. She had let go of anger, guilt, regret, fear, and past resentments. She had finally found something she loved doing. Surfing and bodyboarding was a pastime that helped her stay focused within the present moment. *(If you doubt this then I encourage you to ride a wave.)* This fun pastime helped her practice and develop her own rational self-interest. The result of following her dream was that she became stronger in other areas of her life. Key areas that benefitted from staying in the moment. She began to make healthier decisions. Her life improved with each healthy decision. Her toxic relationship with her narcissist was invalidated by her new growth. Your task is to find *your sacred pastime*. Find your bliss and then do it. Find the activity that reinforces your present moment focus skills. Pursue the activity that you can *lose yourself* within. Once you accomplish this your life will begin to change for the better. The activity does not have to be physical, it can be reading, writing, art, poetry, photography, or social media. The activity is whatever you choose to love and allow into your awareness. Whatever you choose as your expression.

You have the power to create new connections. New life experiences become new connections. New connections become a new pathway.

Learn to choose what you love to do, regardless of the opinion of other people. Listen to the whisperings of your heart. You must learn to recover your humanity for it is the source of your passion and inspiration. We work as humans to pay bills and to live within the world. However we dance, we sing, we pursue photography, we write poetry and music, we explore nature, and we seek expression in fun and within hobby's *because we are human.* These things we love to do are direct messages from our subconscious, guiding us to purpose. Guiding us to happiness, leading us to the truth of our being, leading us to real freedom. Guiding us away from toxic enmeshment within the sick, twisted, abusive culture of narcissism. **Consider the positive possibilities.**

If life is not as you choose, make new choices regarding your life.

I want you to follow her example. I challenge you to begin the path towards your personal and spiritual bliss. I challenge you to begin doing what you love and loving what you do. I want you to begin exercising your freedom of choice muscle. I want you to find those things you loved to do or think you might love to do. Did you ever want to surf or skydive? Hike, camp, ride a mountain bike? Write a book? Learn a foreign language? Do you love working out? What about becoming a fitness trainer and leading others towards a healthy lifestyle? How about being a chef? Do you enjoy reading, swimming, and espresso coffee? *When you leave the narcissistic prison behind you have a golden opportunity to choose again, to create a new reality. You possess the power to re-create. Regardless if that prison was a mental construct created by a vampire, yourself, or others with your full permission, you can remodel your reality.*

You had freedom from choice with the narcissist; you have freedom of choice now. What will you do?

You have the freedom to create a new life, a new reality. You can focus on your children. If you desire you can get a new and different job, you can work two jobs, you have that choice. The narcissist controlled and limited your choices because you either allowed it to happen or you were conditioned in childhood to accept narcopathic manipulation. The creature drained your energy, time, and emotions. The monster is not sorry and will never be sorry about its actions. Leeches just love to suck blood. You can disconnect from the leech. You can reclaim your energy and emotional balance. You can work at night, go to school during the day or do the reverse. You can find something that creates passion in your life and makes you feel inspired. You have the power to follow that inspiration. You can choose to live life differently. *You can choose again.* You can also choose to take the path to destruction and do a life sentence with a toxic vampire on the installment plan. You can choose pain. You can choose to stay within abusive, pestilent relationships. You can choose to ignore the constant drain on your humanity. You can possibly abuse drugs and alcohol just to stay numb in order to cope with your new "normal." You can stay enmeshed within a toxic narcissistic relationship. You can ignore reality. You can ignore positive options that will enhance your growth and development. You can choose to stay manipulated, angry, and allow guilt, anger, and regret to manage and direct your life for you. You can choose to take the path right back into the narcissists psychological prison. You can accept the negative reality that the vampire has created for you and himself. You can willingly return to be the cooperative prisoner of the narcissist. *You can go right back to freedom from choice and make that your comfort zone.*

It is all your choice and it's all up to you.

I challenge you to create a list. This will be the only exercise for this chapter. It will be harder than it seems. I want you to write down one hundred things you would like to experience. It does not matter if you have done some of these things, or if they are things you only dreamed of doing. I have only two conditions and two considerations for what you decide to put on your list. The **two conditions** are: (1) they must be legal, and (2) they must be fun. They can be dreams of childhood or secret dreams and desires you had inside the narcissistic relationship. As you create this list I challenge you to be as Henry David Thoreau put it; "*Independent of the good opinion of others.*" What you put on your list can be expensive, free, or inexpensive. **The two major considerations are:** (1) do not think about the narcissist even once as you create this list, (2) *allow your heart to lead you.*

The past is dead, you are not your past. The future has not yet happened. You have only the present moment, moment to moment, and your choices within each moment will become your future. Seeing this process can begin growth in a new direction. Consider the positive possibilities. You had freedom from choice while enmeshed within the narcissistic relationship, you have freedom of choice now. What will you do with freedom of choice?

The List.

I have included my current list for your consideration as an example. This is not my first list. I have completed many lists. I have completed some things on my current list and am in process of completing others. As you go through the journey of life and encounter lessons you will make choices and out of those choices you will change and grow. Your list will change and grow right along with you. As you experience life events free of the vampire's drama, things that were once important to you may lose importance. Other desires that you thought were trivial or even impossible may come to the forefront and become important. The foremost idea behind this exercise is that you *choose these desires. You practice making healthy, positive choices.*

Something that may seem small and insignificant today may pull at your heart years later.

It is important to honor desire because desire is your inner self guiding you. It is in knowing the importance of small things that we gain an appreciation for the larger things in life that come our way. Once lost inside the narcissistic drama infused life, it is easy to lose communication with your inner self. *This is not a trivial exercise*. I consider it one of the most important exercises in this workbook. If you cannot make life affirming choices, you are essentially an emotional cripple. There is nothing trivial or "funny" about this exercise. Your inability to make healthy, positive, life affirming choices landed you in a narcissistic relationship. By your very own choices you ended up with the boot of a monster upon your neck. You were so incapable of making healthy choices that you put yourself in a situation where a very predictable, self-centered idiot made your choices for you. Your family possibly suffered with you. *This list is no joke when done honestly, for it is a powerful roadmap created entirely by your heart that will guide you to freedom.*

This exercise is about freedom of choice, *not freedom from choice*. This exercise is about you controlling your brain, your body's biological computer, *not your computer controlling you.* Now is not the time to lie to yourself about your relational situation with a vampire. Your life has many possible choices in store for you. The list will lead you out of a situation where your choices are governed by false mental constructs that are decided and dictated by a vampire. You are on a leash that is being controlled by a monster. A creature that only wants to direct your life towards its feeding bowl. You are not free yet; you are becoming free. Until you are independent of the opinion of the vampire you are still manipulated by the vampire. Your life choices are critical now because they will determine your future. ***Begin to choose wisely and make your first list.*** Take your first real steps towards a true and lasting personal freedom. *A real freedom.* You have this present moment to make a map, *so allow the whisperings of your heart to make a good one.* Don't copy mine unless there is something on it you like.

There is no magic way to earn self-esteem, there is only one true way to gain it, you must set goals and accomplish those goals.

1. Go hiking.

2. Go bowling.

3. Learn to create better Haiku.

4. Finish my book of poetry.

5. Eat at Orso's

6. Update my Facebook status which I never seem to do.

7. Climb stairs.

8. Go fishing.

9. Go camping.

10. Learn how to recognize even more thinking errors.

11. Play darts.

12. Hike Table Mountain.

13. Go to Kaladi Brothers coffee and just hang out with my laptop.

14. Go to a book store.

15. Go to Organic Oasis for a vegan meal.

16. Visit Homer.

17. Write more poetry.

18. Take another course on logic.

19. Go to a spoken word event.

20. Speak at a spoken word event.

21. Practice Archery.

22. Visit Seattle.

23. Spoil my Grandson.

24. Spoil my Granddaughter.

25. Listen to Mozart

26. Rent a DVD.

27. Ride a fat tire bike.

28. Visit Eklutna Lake.

29. Meditate.

30. Build a bonfire on the beach.

31. Get better at Spanish.

32. Write in my journal more often.

33. Body board at Crescent Beach again.

34. Practice logic.

35. Listen to Beethoven.

"Our job is to straighten out our own lives."

- Joseph Campbell

36. Buy a CD.

37. Take my wife out dancing.

38. Write a chapter outline.

39. Go to a play.

40. Volunteer.

41. Subscribe to a magazine I really like.

42. Start a blog.

43. Build a driftwood house on the beach.

44. Watch a sunset.

45. Take more pictures.

46. Cruise around in my truck drinking Kaladi Brothers coffee and listening to music.

47. Take a hike around a new lake.

48. Go to Red Chair Café.

49. Call my mom.

50. Picnic and grill at Finger Lake.

51. Camp at Finger Lake.

52. Take pictures at Finger Lake.

53. Take pictures of Salmon.

54. Take pictures of what beavers do to trees.

55. Paint on canvas.

56. Take pictures of Mirror Lake.

57. Laze around on my day off drinking coffee and reading the Sunday paper.

58. Post pictures on Facebook.

59. Beach comb.

60. Take a pottery class.

61. Watch a self-hypnosis video.

62. Hike with a friend.

63. Work out on my heavy bag.

64. Take a first aid course.

65. Take a software class.

66. Drink a protein shake every day.

67. Visit the Funny River.

68. Plant a garden.

69. Visit Seward.

70. Listen to jazz.

71. Go on a road trip.

Something that may seem small and insignificant today may pull at your heart years later.

72   Visit Amsterdam.

73   Visit Hawaii.

74   Body board South Beach.

75   Go to Marine World.

76   Go to a concert.

77. Hang a hammock at the beach and spend the night.

78. Cook salmon over a fire on the beach.

79. Eat at the Rain Forest café.

80. Spend the day in Berkeley.

81. Go to the aquarium at Seward.

82. Paraglide.

83   Read about an ancient culture.

84. Body board with my wife.

85. Take pictures of moose.

86. Read the collected works of Poe.

87. Use a sauna.

88. Visit a game preserve.

89. Visit Talkeetna.

90. Visit Alyeska.

91. Explore the Kenai Peninsula.

92. Pick wild blueberries.

93. Build a home gym.

94. Watch my son drumming.

95. Go to the Artic Man Festival.

96. Take my wife out to an early morning breakfast.

97. Listen to a lecture by Christopher Hitchens.

98. Watch a Star Wars marathon with friends.

99. Make soap with my wife.

100. Hike downtown Anchorage.

Learn to choose what you love to do, regardless of the opinion of other people. Listen to the whisperings of your heart. The past is dead; you are not your past. The future has not yet happened. You have only the present moment, moment to moment, and your choices within each moment will become your future. Seeing this process can begin growth in a new direction.

Now make *your* list. This will be one of the best things you can do for yourself. Making this list will help you remember things you have long forgotten about or gave up on ever doing. This is a chance to make your own choices independent of the narcissists input. This list can rekindle hope and act as a roadmap to a better life.

Do you want to go back to college or trade school? Put it on the list. List your long and short-term goals. Start making **wise choices.** When you are done post your list.

On your wall, on your refrigerator, place it somewhere obvious and locate it so that you see it several times a day. Make it the first thing you see upon waking up and the last thing you see before bed. If you are still enmeshed within the vampire's toxic web, then keep this list secret but assessable only to you. This list is yours alone.

Choose wisely.

You are not your past.

You are not your anger.

Consider the positive possibilities.

The only action you can take in the present moment is to accept the past and its lessons, learn from those lessons and move on. Any other action allows the past to rule your present moment and all you have is your present moment. Regret is a time bandit. Don't allow regret to rob you of your present moment in time.

Remember what you loved before you ever became a prisoner within the narcissist driven relationship.

The past is dead, you are not your past. The future has not yet happened. You have only the present moment, moment to moment, and your choices within each moment will become your future. The narcissist will always talk more than he will listen, it's always "go time" for the vampire because all communication is a contest. The narcissist cannot control his toxic impulses. The narcissist is always right and everyone else is always wrong because the vampire's ego is in charge. If the vampire's position falls, the ego falls along with the vampire's twisted position. The monster wants to remove your freedom of choice. Throughout all this time you have actually had many choices. Many more choices are in store for you. The choices will never stop. Lessons will continue until learned. Einstein's definition of insanity was to do the same thing over and over expecting a different result. You cannot "fix" the monster.

Recovery after narcissistic abuse may not be easy but you are worth the effort. You deserve the inner peace and self-growth that comes from freeing yourself from the abuser. No one has the right to close you off from the experience of self-reflection, happiness, and personal fulfillment. Hold yourself accountable and commit to the work it takes to gain and maintain your personal freedom.

Regaining control over your life is a sacred goal worth your best efforts. Investing your energy into yourself is very rewarding and healing. It is so much better than feeding an energy leech. You are on a sacred journey towards wholeness. You are creating a new life that will be much different than the prison you find yourself in currently. You cannot "fix" the vampire, but you can create a new way of life for yourself. You are worth it. You are the child of an unlimited cosmos. Never forget that fact.

Chapter Four Affirmations: *I am a present moment master and my wise choices reflect this fact.*

I make life affirming choices easily.

I can set strong boundaries.

I like to learn new concepts.

I am open to new ideas.

I create my new reality.

My thoughts and opinions matter.

I am independent of the opinions of other people.

Chapter Five.

Presenting yourself to the world.

You have had some life lessons. Some were due to conditions beyond your control. Some are due to unwise choices. Accept the lessons learned and resolve to make healthy choices in the only place you can choose to do so: the present moment. You only have the present moment, moment to moment, in which to make change and decisions. You cannot change the past, you are not yet in the future, you have only this moment. When you meet new people, you will have only that present moment in time to present yourself. Your choices in language, dress, speech, body language, tone of voice, and facial expressions, will convey an image. That image will be interpreted as "you" by the new people meeting you for the first time. Choose wisely when you present yourself (YOUR-SELF) to the world. You have only the present moment, use that moment in time extremely well.

Abusers in general and narcissists in particular wear different "masks" every day. However, the person living with the narcissist also wears many masks. Within the toxic narcissistic dynamic each person chooses to project an image of themselves to others around them. There are some very basic, human reasons for this behavior. Fear, and a desire for acceptance are two powerful reasons. Deep down you were afraid that you were not smart enough, strong enough, aggressive enough, or clever enough. You made these subconscious decisions living within the narcissist's world you had chosen to inhabit each day. You had a desire to love and be loved by someone. The narcissist needs to feed on your energy, both negative and positive. The vampire can only manipulate your feelings with your permission. This is how it obtains what it desires. This toxic dynamic was a true circle of fear, intimidation, manipulation, and hatred. The answer to the mystery of life for the narcissist is to project an image that others will react to. Fear, pity, desire, victimhood, or false projections as needed will do for the abusive narcissist. Inside the Narcopath driven relationship, fear, pity, desire, and respect, or lack thereof are all things that go great together. This chaos driven life is a narcissists dream. In fact, none of these things are really part of a healthy relationship dynamic.

Fear can result in you being put right back into the cage that the narcissist has created for you. The minions of chaos love psychological cages. Within the narcissistic relationship, dependency is encouraged and sustained by the toxic narcissistic relationship process. By allowing yourself to become a source of energy and narcissistic supply, you are automatically placed within a category by the vampire. The narcissist will demand your life energy along with a form of twisted solidarity and loyalty. His pathology demands nothing less. Your basic humanity is being consumed every day. Just know that being human has nothing to do with this unhealthy relationship so don't try to fix the destructive dynamic. The nasty, abusive manipulations will only strengthen this enforced division between your authentic self and your basic humanity even further. The projections and assertions of the narcissist are a survival skill for the vampire. The monster's grip upon your life is reinforced with posturing, threats, shaming language, violence, gas-lighting, and triangulations. Manipulative affiliations with your friends, family, and various recruited flying monkeys are to be expected. If you allow this un-natural and evil relationship to remain it will never change. This abusive dynamic is not "fixable." *One of your biggest challenge in freeing yourself will lie within how you communicate and present yourself to others both during the narcissistic relationship and after its termination.*

Peace is not merely a distant goal that we seek,

But a means by which we arrive at that goal.

- Martin Luther King, Jr.

If you choose to present yourself to others still wearing your old, outdated, vampire approved mask you only put yourself at risk socially. The mask that served you well within the confines of being a food source for the narcissist will do you nothing good while interacting with other people. You must learn how to be "you" again, even at the mall, the workplace, school, or the gym. As long as you wear that old mask you will instantly be identified and categorized as a "supply source" by the nearest narcopath. You become an instant target for narcissists looking to discard their old supply, triangulate, monkey branch, and become somebody's new "Soul mate." This old, outdated mask will alienate you from the mainstream and stop you from meeting mentally healthy people who might just possibly be human beings. You will be at risk because it is not safe to present yourself to society like a co-dependent, super empathic food source with the sign "Feed upon me" just beneath your surface. Please consider the fact that seventy percent of communication is non-verbal. Your facial expressions and blended micro-expressions speak volumes to those around you. Over time, being in an abusive relationship sculpts you like clay. The minions of chaos love fresh clay.

First let's clear up some misconceptions about how the world values people. *Both narcissists and their prisoners are seen as unbalanced individuals. They are both perceived as victimized, helpless, immature, emotionally crippled people.* Once identified, most mentally healthy people do not respect narcissists, they pity them. Like severe sociopaths, most people may fear them, but they don't respect them. Sometimes they also see the victims of narcissistic abuse as people to be pitied, not respected. The victims of narcopaths may be viewed as people who created their own misery. This is because most psychologically healthy people would tell a narcissist to "get lost" in a hot minute. Pity and fear can cost you a lot within a free society. Potential friends, employers, co-workers, and others may worry that you do not possess the ability to set healthy boundaries. Inside the narcissist free world, respect and self-esteem come to you the old-fashioned way; you set goals and you accomplish those goals. *The narcissist free world operates on different standards and ways of thinking. These standards are vastly dissimilar than the virulent and unhealthy ways of thinking you may have accepted when enmeshed within the nasty narcissistic relationship.*

People in the narcissist- free world admire successful, mentally healthy people and they respect accomplishment. That's why the NHL, NBA, NFL, UFC, and professional boxing are billion-dollar enterprises. Free thinking people admire the beauty and courage of one person facing another in a contest. They pay money to watch this courage. They admire and respect the sportsmanship of pro sports. A narcissistic "expert" with no actual portfolio is seen as someone who is mentally unbalanced. Someone who abusively lives off another's energy by manipulation and deceit are not respected at all. Mentally healthy people loathe and are repulsed by such acts. Respect is never in that equation. Unfortunately, this is reserved for the victims of narcissistic abuse also. Most narcissists are perceived as self-centered idiots by mentally healthy people. This is because mentally healthy people tend to spot manipulative scumbags quickly and easily. Everyone loathes the forty something, know it all, perpetual victim, forever adolescent, manipulative, obvious drama queen or "king." No mentally healthy person wants anything to do with them. You may not like that situation, but I would be lying to you if I implied anything less.

Inside the narcissistic relationship, the forty some-thing, energy leech was accepted or at least tolerated. The perpetual victim could be counted on to accept the narcopaths insanity. The vampire was free to communicate with its victim unencumbered by reason. The emotionally stunted, violent, abusive idiot, always posturing about "respect," was given the attention he craved. Sometimes the creature was accorded deference, and false respect by their current energy source. Never in the narcissist-free world will anyone who acts even remotely like the abusive vampire earn real respect. This will not ever happen. Neither will the victims of these vampires be respected, until they earn that respect by starving the vampire out of their lives. By demonstrating solid, healthy choices you will be respected. Allowing the narcissist to keep control will however "earn" your way right back into a vampire-controlled nightmare. This toxic, self-created prison is not the free world and its abuse driven dynamic cannot prepare you for the narcissist free world. The vampire's prime directive is to gain and maintain control over your life. He wants his supply source and you are his chosen supply. The creature is only following its prime directive. What is your prime directive?

The narcissist will always talk more than he will listen, it's always "go time" for the vampire because all communication is a contest. The narcissist cannot control his toxic impulses. The narcissist is always right and everyone else is always wrong because the vampire's ego is in charge. If the vampire's position falls, the ego falls along with the vampire's twisted position. The vampire will go to extreme lengths to ensure that never happens. The monster wants to remove your freedom of choice. Throughout all this time you have had many choices. Many more choices are in store for you. The choices will never stop. Lessons will continue until learned.

Please remember the following:

The Narcissists motto is "I did not do that."

The Narcissists slogan is "It's never my fault, it's your fault (or someone else's fault) I did that." ("But I still didn't do it.")

The Narcissists oath is "I am never at fault. You asked for it, that's why I did it." ("But I still didn't do it and you're crazy for accusing me."

Start thinking like a true survivor.

The only action you can take in the present moment is to accept the past and its lessons, learn from those lessons

and move on. Any other action allows the past to rule your present moment and all you have is your present moment. If you are in relationship with someone who talks more than they listen, if it's always "go time" for them because all communication is a contest and their ego will always rule their actions, then it is time to reconsider the choices you have made. If they cannot control their impulses, but desire control over you, then you are in danger. If they are always right and everyone else is always wrong, their ego is in charge and you are on your way back to reside within a narcissist ruled prison of your own creation. You cannot yet handle freedom of choice. You must learn to master freedom of choice. Throughout all this time you have had choices. Many more choices are in store for you. The choices will never stop. Lessons will continue until learned.

Your first serious challenge will be to reveal aspects of yourself (your-self) rather than hide aspects of yourself behind a mask to other people. You must stop seeking approval. You will have to learn how to do this in a socially acceptable way. Inside the abusive narcissistic relationship/prison you learned to repress emotions and express others. You learned to hide your feelings and display only those feelings that enhanced the survival of the narcissist and decreased your victimization. Sometimes you learned that giving into the vampire's desires served you better because it decreased your chances of being further harmed emotionally and even physically. You were mistaken. Giving into the narcopath only feeds the creature. The minions of chaos love empathy, it feeds them well.

How you misuse your brain. Your brain is a biological computer. You have an amygdala and a limbic system. You have a dopamine reward system. You have a hypothalamus. They are awesome. Your amygdala has several important jobs, one of them is to remember everything painful and pleasurable you have ever experienced. It does this with an amazing precision. The amygdala operates seven times faster than normal thought. Crazy fast. The amygdala is a catalyst for survival. It is a tool for the "Flight or fight" response. So, it works like this: You see or hear your abuser/narcissist. Your amygdala has seen him seven times faster than your first awareness of his presence. Your limbic system ignites, and your hypothalamus begins pumping out proteins and peptides. These proteins and peptides go straight to your cells that have developed specific receptor sites for them to lock onto, much like keys in a lock. Suddenly you become your emotions. Your biological computer is in charge, not you. Thus, begins a chemical cascade, a domino effect. The first domino is pushed over by your biological computer and the rest fall with no effort on your part. You become a willing participant in an exercise in stupidity, futility, psychological pain, and ignorance. The dance of the narcissist and his supply source/victim begins anew. The narcissist is not the only one in the relationship "Staying ready so he won't have to get ready." The narcissist victim is in "Fight or flight" mode 24-7. The victim develops a hyper-awareness of tone of voice, body language, and the vampire's many moods. Many narcissist survivors finally leave. They do so with well-developed PTSD.

You are not your past.

You are not your anger, your fear, your feelings, or your emotions.

Consider the positive possibilities.

Anger is a secondary emotion always. You choose to be angry. Your response is all yours. You cannot control what others do and say in the moment, but you have total control over what you do and say within that one precious moment in time. If you constantly "stay ready so you don't have to get ready, "in order to deal with your vampires predations the only thing you are ready for is a self-created prison cell with your chosen narcissist as the warden.

The only real challenge we face is the mastery of our thoughts.

How to use your brain.

Know that whenever you feel an emotion you are feeling the action of a protein or peptide, released by your hypothalamus because of your amygdala and limbic system. Giving in to this emotion in a negative, submissive, or destructive way is akin to allowing your laptop computer to dictate your life and your immediate actions. Only a person with no understanding of their ability to control themselves would do that. You have control. Truly free people do not allow their biological computer to rule their actions. They think before they act regardless of their personal feelings within the moment. This is called impulse control and emotional regulation. It is a beautiful thing and it is one of the functions of your frontal lobes. You are "living" within a narcissist's food chain because you have impulse control challenges that involve making healthy decisions. You have the power to think clearly before you speak, make choices, or act. The narcissist has the exact same psychological challenges except he is pathologically survival centered. The abuser also has the "luck" of the psychopath. The vampire is "guilt free." Lacking compassion or empathy he is free to act out his instinct driven behavior with no care or concern over the pain he inflicts upon others. His prime directive is control. He must secure and lock down his energy source. The vampire's motives are always instinct driven, and inherently selfish. The narcissist can only mimic emotion. This is a tool he employs to trap his prey. If your motivation is always hoping for an unattainable future with your chosen narcissist, you are living in a nightmare. You are in a real-life horror movie and thinking it's a dream world. This level of denial will always cause you to fail at mental clarity. Living in delusion to cope with abuse will crush your life. You will not be able to think things through; thus you cannot foresee possible negative outcomes or possible *positive alternatives.*

Throughout all this time you have had choices. Many more choices are in store for you. The choices will never stop. Lessons will continue until learned.

Please remember: It is very easy to tell if you are not in control of your biological computer. If you are easily manipulated, and you bleed positive and negative energy freely for your toxic vampire you need to re-examine your life. If everything becomes an argument because all communication is a contest you have become food for an energy leech. The narcissist is an expert at the art of mis-direction. The abuser is adept at directing your thoughts in such a way that you believe you are doing what you want to do. In reality you are only doing what he wants you to do. If you constantly show up late for your work and obligations or appointments due to conflicts with your narcissist, he is in control. If you find that you must "defend" yourself constantly regarding your free will actions and choices, then you have dysfunctional, abusive, and possibly narcissistic relationship challenges. If you spend your day engaging in multiple, twenty-minute, ego fueled arguments with someone who finds fault in everyone you communicate with, and everything you do, these are red narcissistic relationship flags. If anger, manipulation, shaming language, hatred, and resentment are the "fuel" in your significant others gas tank, then his or her abusive pathology is in total control. If the vampires wicked infection oversees all relational communication, it is time to run. The minion of chaos is in control of your life as well as your biological computer.

Please remember the following: (I am going to keep on repeating it.)

The Narcissists motto is "I did not do that."

The Narcissists slogan is "It's never my fault, it's your fault (or someone else's fault) I did that." (But I still didn't do it.)

The Narcissists oath is "I am never at fault. You asked for it, that's why I did it." ("But I still didn't do it and you're crazy for accusing me."

Narcissistic thinking is toxic, self-centered centered thinking always. That is why everyone else is "wrong" except the soul crushing vampire. This type of interaction with psychologically healthy people in the narcissist-free world will exhaust them mentally and they will simply shun the narcissist. Grey rock/no contact is the natural response of a healthy person once they realize that they are under narcissistic assault. If you continue to allow yourself to be a supply source for a narcissist you will be treated like a narcissist yourself. You will be denied opportunity and you won't even know what the opportunity was in the first place. No one will reach out to you in friendship except for other damaged, emotionally stunted, co-dependent people. If you don't change this dynamic, you are just heading back into the narcissistic relationship cage. *If you want to change other people's opinions, show them rather than tell them. To be an example always requires choice.*

"Your past is only an ancient reflection of old choices invalidated by new growth within the present moment."

Narcissists fail to succeed in entrapping healthy people and are kicked to the curb in basically two ways: **they try to fool themselves and they try to fool others**. They violate the two survival guidelines that you should aspire to follow within the narcopath free world environment. It will be challenging at first for you to make these guidelines a lifestyle habit on a healthy continuum. These two guidelines might feel unsafe and uncomfortable for you after years of narcissistic abuse and a vampire fueled relationship. Do not expect perfection right away, the most important thing you can do is to make a sincere effort to follow these guidelines every day. Just relax and try. Accountability is a strength. Accountability is something that the minions of chaos avoid at all costs. Accountability is bright and clear. It is the natural domain of healthy people.

1. Do not try to fool yourself.

Narcissists believe most of their own lies and deceptions. It may "work" for them short term but this is not healthy. In the narcissistic relationship you aspired to survive. You questioned yourself and told yourself things would get better. They never improved. There was no chance that they would. You remembered the "good times" and you hoped they would return. You had little mantras always going off in your mind like *"She had a horrible childhood"* or *"It's not his fault, he didn't really*

mean it," or "She was abused." This was the ideal way of surviving within the pain of a narcissistic relationship. Coping measures used generally involved the victim displaying acceptance, humor, and deception. Your true feelings were always repressed. All with the unconscious goal of enabling narcissistic manipulation. It was beneficial for the narcissist to be a little unpredictable and to have people afraid of him, pity him, or just be "on his side." You, along with the always recruited "flying monkeys" were just puppets. Tools used to feed the abusive vampire. The narcissist is an expert at walking that thin line between compliance with authority and non-compliant, manipulative aggression. The abuser may use passive aggression however the goal is the same. The vampire is thirsty, and it wants your energy. You fooled yourself into accepting all this toxic garbage as your new "Normal" and it became your life. Dysfunction became the daily routine.

To present yourself without a mask that the narcissist approved of was perceived as aggression, non-compliance, and competition. This is not the reality of the narcissist free world and you must survive and thrive within this world. If you hang on to the past and insist upon wearing your old, useless, dysfunctional mask you will be perceived as toxic. Your old mask only displays you as a maladjusted or immature person in the free world. You will spend a lot of your time alone and miserable. When not being alone and miserable you can count on attracting Narcissistic, abusive, damaged, dysfunctional people with criminal and addictive thinking errors into your life. In a very short amount of time they will quickly lead you into chaos, stupidity, and ultimately, unhappiness. But don't worry, you can always blame "them" and stay lost in the chaos you create by your choices. Living up to the ideals of the narcissist and cooperating with his dysfunctional impulses will negatively impact your life. You can choose an entirely new life that is always available to you in the narcissist free world. Allowing yourself to be an energy source for a vampire can strangle friendships before they happen. It can stifle job interviews. It can close you off to better times and better people in your life. *You will attract the negativity you accept into the world you create for yourself.* It does not have to be like that.

The mask you wore with the narcissist, the mask that helped feed the vampire, this very mask can attract another narcissist and put you right back in the narcissistic relationship prison. It can do this time and time again. Dump that mask. It's a survival situation.

2.   Do not try to fool everyone.

You really won't fool everyone forever so why try in the first place? Avoid the drama, lies, deceit, and personal embarrassment guaranteed to eventually come your way. Make the decision to just be real with yourself and everyone else. Inside the narcissistic relationship you became conditioned to a lifestyle based upon living with a dysfunctional, maladapted, abusive, manipulative idiot. This monster was convinced that he was fooling you and all other people within his web. You also attempted to fool everyone all the time. No one wants to admit they were vampire food. The narcissist is pathologically prepared to manipulate your friends, counselors, case managers, teachers, co-workers, family members, and anyone within your life. Basically everyone within your contained and confined, freedom from choice, negative, narcissist driven universe. These choices mirrored the narcissist's instinct driven behaviors. You both probably resented each other's behaviors for different reasons, possibly at different times, and you both achieved different outcomes. *Don't try to duplicate within your new life after the narcissist your old reality from the past narcissistic relationship.* If you think this will work just check the healing rate for narcissists. They are incurable. No one fools everyone all the time. Trust me, narcissists are not a novelty to healthy people. People involved with narcissistic drama are perceived as willing victims and clueless about life by society in general. You have the power to grow past your old way of life. You don't need your abuser.

Narcissists think they are fooling people. They were always right and everyone else was stupid, clueless, and always wrong. They were one superior, energy consuming vampire. They don't fool healthy people.

You kept the narcissists dirty secrets. You engaged with the vampire over stupid and petty conflicts. You allowed toxic mind games just for the fun and amusement of the vampire playing them. You accepted the daily drama. You fooled others about the true nature of your relationship with the monster. You fooled people about your very lack of happiness, and your toxic lifestyle inside the relationship. Your cooperation with the monster enabled him to feed upon your energy. Worse, it enabled him to recruit your friends and family against you. You fooled yourself.

You accepted the new "normal" of the narcissist driven life. Eventually you knew he was *lying to anyone who would listen about life with you. You also came to realize that he was being dishonest about almost everything in his past.* Meanwhile you were lying to yourself about a future that your present choices doomed from ever manifesting. This life of lies and continual destructive life choices became a habitual ritual that hardwired itself into your mind. You became "vampire conditioned." You became an energy supply for a monster. No one could ever make your vampire "wrong." If anyone challenged the obvious lies they were "disrespecting" your narcissist and it was "go time" for him. The minions of chaos love to "stay ready, so they don't have to get ready." Instant defense mode leading to attack mode is their "normal." You accepted this drama because over time you had come to accept the narcissistic, contest driven communication as normal. Your role within your own self-deception was never something you considered because you could never be "so wrong." You were only being "Understanding." Your self-deception had to be maintained, even if it meant allowing a monster to feed upon your energy. After all he (or she) was your "soul mate" and you "loved" the vampire at one point. You remembered the "good times." You fell in love with the illusion, not the reality.

Your self-esteem has taken a severe beating after life with the narcopath. You have the power to gain it all back. Creating a new and powerful reality is part of your skill-set. You must set goals and begin the work to attain those goals. You have had some harsh life lessons. Some lessons were due to situations outside of your control, (family members and upbringing for example.) Some life lessons were due to unwise choices on your part. The past is dead, and it only lives on inside your mind. You can accept the lessons you have learned. See the lessons as gifts. Resolve to make healthy choices within the present moment. You only have the present moment so use it with discernment. You have the power to make and sustain healthy change in your life. You have the strength of wise decisions to sustain your growth. There are positive possibilities in front of you just waiting for you to claim them. No one can change the past so let it go. Your present moment decisions create your future so create a powerful future for yourself. You have only this moment and you can use it wisely. Use your precious and finite moments to create a future of freedom from abuse. You will meet new people. You will eventually have to present yourself to others. Your choices in how you choose to speak will convey an image about you to the new people you meet. You have the power to reinvent yourself. You deserve a "do-over." We all do. I have had the privilege of witnessing countless inmates and clients re-create themselves. I owe them so much because they made me a true believer. I have a massive and unrelenting faith in the power of the human spirit to overcome adversity. I have seen fierce effort bear results. I can never forget the transformations I have seen. I am thankful for the gifts of my own lessons as well as the lessons of others shared with me.

New choices will come your way. These opportunities will impact your future as well as the present. Please remember: Allowing your past to rule your present moment choices will lead only to despair. It was your vampire who made everyone "wrong" and itself always "right." Do not allow the past to dictate your present. If you do you will win every battle and lose the ultimate war for your freedom. Even when you are free of the abusive idiot, you will still be mentally trapped. You will think like a victim and act like a victim. You will eventually return to the place where victims live out their lives. All of it will reflect your choices. You are not a victim so don't make choices like a victim.

Expressing yourself well is a key survival tactic. It is a tactic that can help you survive the antics of the minions of chaos by enhancing your ability to communicate. Healthy communication can help you connect with healthy people. Outside the dysfunctional walls of the narcissistic relationship wholesome communication will help you reach out and create a support network. Being assertive, not aggressive, is the norm for drama free and vampire free people. Aggressive, verbally assaultive, angry, manipulative, narcopathic people, eventually wind up on law enforcement's radar. This is because the free world is generally designed for idiots to be located and neutralized. After all, it is law enforcement's job to notice angry, aggressive, dysfunctional people. This is what they train to do as a career choice. Eventually and hopefully these narcopathic people end up living in a cage where they eat food prepared by other angry, aggressive, unhappy, dysfunctional narcopathic people. They also regularly use the toilet two feet from their bunk.

Do not allow the Narcopaths deadly games to ensnare you or destroy your life. Once you see reality you may have an urge to fight with your abuser. Don't end up eating bad food and using the toilet two feet from your bunk. Avoid having to defecate in front of a beady eyed, aggressive, manipulative, emotionally stunted cell "partner." Learn to be assertive and not aggressive. Do not mirror your narcissist's behavior by adapting your communication style to match his or her chaos driven lifestyle. Dysfunctional, contest driven, win-lose communication errors only lead to a mental or physical cage eventually. *Unless you like that lifestyle and communication style of course, no judgment.*

The past is dead; you are not your past. The future has not yet happened. You have only the present moment, moment to moment, and your choices within each moment will become your future. Seeing this process can begin growth in a new direction. Consider the positive possibilities. You accepted freedom from choice inside

the dysfunctional, narcissistic relationship, you have freedom of choice now. What will you do?

You start with being polite to people. This is not weakness. The Harvard of bodyguard schools, Executive Security International, teaches its students a course on international relations and manners. Well trained bodyguards are dangerous and resourceful people. They are also polite and calm. They use assertive speech, never aggressive speech, they are soft spoken generally. They solve dangerous situations without violence about ninety nine percent of the time. When I went through the course my instructors drilled an important mantra into my consciousness: *"If you have to use violence you did something wrong."* Loud and aggressive speech is violent speech. It sets the literal tone for violent escalation. Rude and combative speech places you immediately in the verbal and posturing phase of conflict. The action phase is the next phase. Don't go there if you can possibly avoid going there. Don't allow yourself to be led there either.

Practice being polite every day. Smile at people. Say thank you to the lady that rings up your order at the grocery store. Look people in the eye and be pleasant. Practice being non-confrontational. Speak quietly when possible. Use your "I" statements. "I see that you are stressed." "I feel that you are being unfair in this situation." "I really want to communicate with you without profanity." I know this is not a real option with the narcissistic idiot all the time, and silence may be a better option. If you are communicating with social service authorities, police, court officials, and others, being assertive and not aggressive is an important skill for you to grasp. Healthy (and unhealthy) communication impacts your continued mental health and possibly your continued freedom. Narcissists love to manipulate agencies and people, don't play into the narcissist's twisted game. Communicate like the human you really are.

Einstein's definition of insanity was to do the same thing over and over expecting a different result.

You will have to speak to people every day within the narcissist free world that you eventually create. You will have to interact with others to survive socially. If you want to thrive interaction will be mandatory. Humans are social creatures and social interaction is a necessary part of life. You will speak thousands of words each day, so don't just throw out words. Never take for granted that others will automatically understand how you feel or what you desire. Never take any communication with others for granted. You have become accustomed to narcissistic patterns of communication. The vampire has infected you with its poison. Don't allow the narcissists vile ways of communicating to become yours. You have become used to exchanging the vile coin minted by the monster. You accepted the toxic exchange rate he set. You have no idea how poisonous your communication has become. Try to remember that harsh words once spoken can rarely be taken back.

Please remember: The past is dead; you are not your past. The future has not yet happened. You have only the present moment, moment to moment, and your choices within each moment will become your future. Seeing this process can begin growth in a new direction.

Your tone of voice, facial expressions, body language, and your sentence construction are all under your control. *YOUR COMPLETE CONTROL ALWAYS*. No excuses. Once your words come out of your mouth you cannot retrieve those words. Do not use words as manipulative weapons or camouflage the way the narcopath uses words. That way of communication will lead you back into chaos with people in general and society in particular. You must strive to communicate honestly with others. Just speak straight to people and gauge their responses. You must learn to recognize thinking errors used by narcissists as well as other dysfunctional people and take evasive/corrective action. The narcissistic relationship has crippled your ability to speak honestly and straightforward to people and you may not be aware of this. Narcissists pathologically avoid most healthy communication. Honest engagement with normal humans usually does not produce the positive and negative energy the narcopath craves from humanity. Remember that your goal is to avoid remaining in the vampire's malicious relationship any longer. Your goal is to escape the vampires mental prison. You need to adapt to the environment you want to thrive within. Your goal is a personally created new world. A new space that makes it uncomfortable and uninviting for any current or future narcissist to dwell within. An environment that allows you to grow and thrive without vampire driven limits. Your goal is freedom from dysfunction and abuse.

Your choices within the present moment become your future.

There are some excellent ways to improve your ability to speak straightforward and honestly.

1. Never use clichés or slang when you communicate with others, either in writing or verbally. The clear majority of people within society will think you have intelligence challenges or a dull mind. They will simply assume you cannot think for yourself or they will see you as emotionally stunted and immature. Insulting people and constantly communicating in a win-lose manner just causes people to shut down communication. Saying "Um" after every third word as you speak just insures that you look stupid to free people. They will judge you to be inferior and they will treat you that way when it comes to job promotions, interviews, social situations, and upward mobility in general. In the free world clichés, profanity, fallacies of logic, and slang are considered the domain of the ignorant. They are not the clever social skills they are perceived as by abusers. People will assume you are crude,

rude, unbalanced, and unintelligent. They will think you are a minion of chaos. Healthy people try to avoid chaos.

Your past is only an ancient reflection of old choices invalidated by new growth in the present moment.

2.   Try your best to not use unnecessary interjections in your speech to other people. Words like "man," "you know," "uh," only frustrate people who are listening to you. (Or trying to listen to you.) If you use these interjections in your sentences people will eventually tune you out and stop listening. There is no need to be angry over this phenomenon because it is just natural human behavior. People will not listen or give their attention to someone who makes it hard to do so. They will lose focus on what you are trying to communicate to them.

Your biggest challenge post narcissist will lie within how you present yourself to others.

3.   Try to avoid using words you are not comfortable using. You cannot hope to impress anyone with multi-syllable words you just learned yesterday. Strive to remain true to your own natural and personal speech patterns. Don't be "that person," (you know who they are,) the person using complex words incorrectly, oblivious that they are doing so.

Choices are everywhere, and choices impact the future as well as the present.

4.   Try to not choose to use profanity. Sometimes (but not always) the secret life of a narcissist/ sociopath escalates to profanity where it quickly becomes part of the "normal" language. Profanity can be sprinkled throughout everyday conversation. Within the confines of the abusive relationship profanity is rampant and immune to every rule of grammar. Profane words are not just adjectives, they cross all lines and sometimes are used as nouns, verbs, and personal pronouns. They become part of almost all dysfunctional syntax. Profane communication becomes the "norm" and experiences no barriers. Profanity is almost always a challenge for someone re-entering the social network after they leave their narcissist. Eliminating profanity from your daily speech is well worth it when you realize the price of profanity in actual communication. One slip can cost you a job offer, a relationship, or a chance at something new. You will be judged by your speech, you can accept this fact, or you can deny it and lose societal credibility. Worse than profanity however is your own self judgement and condemnation. Please don't allow your communication style to harm your future interactions. Leave it all behind along with your vampire. It is your choice. *Einstein's*

definition of insanity was to do the same thing over and over expecting a different result.

For many people profanity presents a particularly difficult challenge post narcissist/sociopath simply because profanity has become such a strong part of their internal dialog. Profanity and personal insults are expected and accepted in communication. Your biological computer oversees your speech patterns because you have created the connections for it to do so. You will have to create non-profane connections within your biological computer. Lucky for you, connections that are not used grow weak and connections that are used frequently grow strong. Your brain is amazing. You will have to take control and build new connections within your biological computer. New pathways that support and sustain your healthy new growth in a life affirming direction. You must resist and tame the profane urge. There was a time in your life (pre-narcissist) when you did not speak that way. You can make that happen again with some effort. In the free world people will judge you by your speech and the content of your language. They will also judge the content of your character by your speech as well.

You can be upset about the role language and communication play in relationships and in the social world. You can whine, play the victim, argue about "freedom of speech" and resist the truth. If you have been struggling within a long term, toxic, narcissistic relationship you have communication challenges. You have learned to communicate with the narcissist on his dysfunctional terms. Otherwise the vampire would have discarded you long ago because he would not be able to feed. His toxic communication abilities are his greatest weapons. This is the main reason that going "no contact" works with severe narcissists. Think before you speak. Hasty words can be as damaging as hasty bullets. *Words are powerful. Use them wisely and with discretion.*

Your choices within the present moment become your future.

5. Stop communicating like the narcissist by ceasing or severely limiting interaction with the narcissist. Avoid talking "down" to people the way the narcissist denigrated you. On the same note, try to avoid talking "up" to people. Within a free society both practices are regarded as insecurity within the speaker. In free society people who stand for nothing are perceived as being weak and the common view is that anything will knock them over. Alternately, while it is important to have an opinion, those who try to force their opinion upon others who may not agree with that opinion are regarded as manipulative, negative, pushy, unintelligent, and insecure people. Whenever you can, practice speaking in a simple, straightforward manner. Use as few words as possible to communicate

your position. Try to create sentences that are concise, yet information packed. Use the fewest words possible to convey your message. I recommend that you read a novel by Earnest Hemingway entitled "The Old Man and The Sea" for sentence construction examples.

Pay attention to how he constructs some of his sentences. They tend to be short, concise and information packed sentences. Simple sentences carrying complex thoughts are respected by healthy people. They don't waste time and they pack a lot of information. *Uncluttered language, free of overt manipulation, logical fallacies, and profanity, is powerful language. People tend to listen to this kind of communication and respond well to it because it keeps their attention.* Don't clutter your language and communication with rude adjectives or needless "figures of speech." Communication does not have to be a contest that engages your fight or flight response. In short, communicate as if you never interacted with your narcissist. For the minion of chaos, communication was (and always will be) a competition. You learned to communicate with that vampire and accept its vile terms. It is important to realize that healthy people don't communicate the way you were trained to communicate. When the vampire ruled your life chaos, despair and dysfunction ruled your internal dialog. This negative payload influenced how you perceived the world and how you spoke to people. Pay attention to your body language, facial expressions, and tone of voice as you speak. Speaking well to others is a powerful skill.

Learn to use this effectively. If possible, record yourself on video when speaking. Then watch and listen closely to your true communication skills. A video recording can be brutal in its detached honesty. This will help you correct the most blatant errors in your speech. Often a person has no idea how they present themselves to the world. Watching yourself speak can be a great help in becoming a good, effective communicator.

When you meet new people, you will have only that present moment in time to present yourself. Your choices in language, speech, body language, tone of voice, and facial expressions, will convey an image. That image will be interpreted as "you" by the new people meeting you for the first time. Choose wisely when you present yourself (YOUR-SELF) to the world. You have only the present moment, spend that precious moment in time extremely well.

Creating and living within a new way of being that only you create can be the best thing you ever do for yourself. Living and interacting with people who only know personal freedom, who have never been drained by a vampire, can be challenging for people recovering from narcissistic abuse. This is because you gradually became used to communicating with a self-centered vampire who held unbalanced expectations. A twisted creature that expected energy and unearned accolades both from you, and society as well. Society does not agree with most of the assumptions, prejudices, expectations, and entitlement mentality that narcissists tend to espouse. Society in general does not feel that narcissists are owed jobs and respect above their abilities. Most of society does not think a minion of chaos is "owed" free housing, medical care, food, clothing, energy, attention or even a second chance at communicating. Society generally thinks that people need to prove themselves to gain and earn opportunities. If you hope to remain free of your current abuser and possible future abusers, you must learn the "rules." (The ones I posted in the very beginning of this book.) In order to survive and thrive within a free society, you will have to know the "rules" and play by those rules. After you escape your Narcopath, you will be exposed to an incredibly complex barrage of people, obligations, responsibilities, and events. How capable you are in dealing with this onslaught will directly affect your personal happiness. You have the power to control how you interact with people, places, and things. Use that power wisely.

Some personal development ideas.

Think about and identify ten reasons why you like yourself. Only write them down if your narcissist will never find them. These reasons will change over time. That is good news.

Name five things you would like to accomplish within the next five years. Include how each of these goals will improve you as a person and better your position within society.

Read "The Old Man and the Sea" by Earnest Hemmingway. Write out some of your thoughts and impressions regarding clutter-free communication.

Chapter Five Affirmations:

I accept the life lessons I have learned.

I effortlessly communicate with others the truth of my being.

I only accept honest and truthful communication because I deserve it.

I communicate well.

I have strong personal boundaries.

Chapter Six

Looking closely at the vampire, review.

Observation and recognition of the abusive patterns and traits of the creature will help you avoid this unbalanced predator both now and in the future. It is worth reviewing narcopath patterns, so let's review. Let us get a little more in depth and explore "Overt" and "Covert" narcissists. Some of this may seem redundant but I encourage you to make the effort for review. It will benefit you in the long run. You must become your own "expert" because the mental health "industry" has generally ignored or betrayed the victims of Narcopaths. The industry has let survivors down on an unhealthy continuum. The "experts" have only led victims into chaos. A chaos that allows the vampires to feed. A systemic chaos that pushes the same old, tired, narrative. The dysfunctional mantra that creatures devoid of compassion and empathy can be taught to become compassionate and empathetic. Worse still, that these predatory monsters can interact with accountability and emotional authenticity. Let's look closely at the vampire. Becoming familiar with its dysfunctional traits is a wise decision. It allows you the power to use your own discernment. Don't worry about "diagnosing" anyone. There are enough people with doctorate degrees messing up that aspect of the mental health industry. Just focus on observation of the abusive dynamic. The goal is to learn to recognize dysfunction and abuse. You need to learn these skills, so you can end abuse now and avoid new abuse later on. The intention is your personal empowerment. From strength you can respond in your own rational self-interest. So, at the risk of being repetitive, let's analyze everything again. Patterns are important because they are powerful tools of identification. Every pattern you learn is a tool that will help you free yourself from the minions of chaos. Together let's fill up our tool chest.

I have been accused of being "insensitive" towards cluster B folks. Narcissists, sociopaths, and borderlines in particular. I wrote this book for the survivors of the minions of chaos. I am not trying to hurt, insult, diagnose, or label anyone. It is my goal to help people empower themselves. However I admit that I do not care if I hurt some people's feelings while in the process of attempting to help the true victims. The minions of chaos want to be able to kick someone in their genitals and then complain that their victim gave them a limp. If empowering the victims of Narcopaths angers some people, too bad.

The stereotypical narcissist is usually perceived as the typical attention addict. They may project a larger than life personality. They typically act like they are media personalities, just without possessing any notable media accomplishments. If you need examples just peruse videos on social media. You will find many platforms filled with people craving attention. Some people on social media are entertaining. Many have messages worth following and content that is worthwhile. The majority are just not worth watching. That is why most social media (for example) only has a few superstars and a lot of boring content. (Just my opinion.) The majority of social media personalities seem to be "experts without portfolio." Your personal narcissist may behave like a Rockstar or a movie star, but it is all projection. The belief that they are "special" exists only within the confines of their unbalanced, emotionally unregulated, predatory mind. They are almost always the "expert" in the room without experience or actual accomplishment. Remember the red flag, if the narcissist is accomplished in some field of study, he will proclaim loudly for all to hear that he is the "Expert." He will announce that his knowledge and understanding trumps all mere mortals. The minions of chaos are always on a sacred quest to draw every bit of attention/energy to themselves. The vampire will behave charismatically or obnoxiously because energy is what the monster craves. Negative or positive, the energy leech does not care. The fiend is a walking, talking fallacy of logic and obvious thinking errors. The vampire will alert your sub-conscious mind and trigger your limbic system. Your amygdala will stay busy with an idiot in your life. It is guaranteed that the vampire will attempt to anger you or charm you. Deep down there will always be the feeling that something is "off" about the narcopath. This is the creature that will captivate, alarm, or insult everyone present in the room. The minion of chaos is always pathologically driven to put forth a great effort to suck every bit of energy/attention his way. Positive attention in the form of admiration is fine, however he will take negative attention also as this will lead to conflict. Thus more energy is directed towards the vampire for his never-ending consumption. However, the narcissist is somewhat more complicated than just the average, over the top attention addict. Narcissists exist along an unhealthy, toxic, continuum of extraversion and introversion, and for every over the top, obnoxious attention craving idiot there are plenty of "quiet" and "shy" Narcissists also. Nasty little vampires feigning innocence and/or perpetual victimhood as they wreak the same or worse havoc as the overt narcissist. In addition, while the sly/covert narcissist may claim innocence, or victim status don't fall for this manipulation. This creature is just as dangerous, selfish, manipulative, and destructive to your life as the overt/obvious narcopath. Don't give into stress over what kind of abuser is in your life. As I stated before, we humans are natural pattern seekers. All narcissists, just like the vampires they emulate, exhibit patterns. These are toxic and obvious patterns that we can recognize and use to avoid interaction with these monsters. Again, don't worry about a label or diagnosis, for even the "Experts" fall short in this area. Just hone your observational and listening skills. It does not matter if someone is "diagnosed," just watch for the patterns of dysfunction, abuse, and manipulation. You won't just avoid narcissists by sharpening your powers of observation. You will also avoid other dysfunctional, negative, abusive idiots who may try to control you in the future. Refuse to allow them to fester like an infected wound within your life.

In my opinion, Narcissistic Personality Disorder (NPD) is part of a serious, dangerous, incurable spectrum disorder. Its pathology is not well understood or universally accepted by "experts." The vampires predations are generally not dealt with constructively by the counseling industry. NPD abuse victims are clearly not understood well by most mental health professionals. If NPD was well understood, then the victims of these vampires might be better cared for. This is just my opinion and I do not expect anyone to agree with me. I do not consider myself an "expert" just a perpetual student of human nature. I believe the victims of these monsters are usually not given the help, understanding, or consideration they deserve. It is the current consensus within the mental health and recovery community's that people who present with NPD present that way due to experiencing a serious, traumatic, psychological/emotional injury or injuries as a child. It is assumed usually to be something involving physical abuse, or emotional abuse such as shame, neglect, loss, or overindulgence by a parent or primary caregiver. Mental health professionals usually rely on the narcissist to report these assertions. It is my opinion that if the narcissist is speaking, he or she is most likely lying or manipulating. According to the current social service mantra, the narcissist's original trauma that caused the wound is never resolved, thus the wound cannot heal. He or she fails to develop any healthy life coping skills. Emotional regulation may be impaired. The victim/narcissist will never develop any mature ability to see beyond his or her toxic, manipulative, neediness. The narcissist will never develop the basic human ability to empathize with others nor the compassion to care for others. The narcissist is seen by most therapists as a perpetual wounded child who needs healing and understanding. Thus, a perpetual victim, not to be held accountable for his or her destructive behavior. Terms like healing the "inner child" are applied to narcissists daily. Narcissists love to play the victim so of course they manipulate freely. They are often assisted (often unintentionally) by the very mental health professionals involved in the toxic situation. This mantra of perpetual victimhood is the official mantra exposed by social service experts daily. In my opinion, the narcissist is a toxic vampire that will never find healing and only cause chaos, pain and dysfunction wherever the creature goes. This book is for the often-unnoticed victims of the vampire. This is a book to help victims increase their observational and listening skills.

I do not perceive the narcissist as a tragic victim within this twisted scenario. After encountering the damage these predators have inflicted upon some of my clients it is very difficult for me to sympathize with these psychic vampires. I also do not believe that all narcissists are "created" by childhood abuse or traumatic events. I believe the causes for narcissism can be due to both nature and nurture, I believe that nature can produce a narcopath on her own. I believe some narcissists are born and some made, and some are a deadly combination of the two. The obvious and documentable, selfishness, inability to care or express empathy for others, along with the unquenchable and pathological demand for attention are all behaviors that are dangerous enough on their own. When you couple these with the ongoing thinking errors things become even more toxic. Add in the pathological lying, the habitually evil and ruthless effort to prop up and defend an unquenchable ego at the expense of all others, and you have an intentionally cruel situation. Narcissists will work their nasty pathology non- stop and without a care for the damage and destruction they cause to other people's lives. These qualities and more make the narcissist/vampire emotionally, psychologically, socially, and sometimes even physically dangerous. These patterns are observable however, and thus action can be taken on a healthy continuum to starve these psychic vampires.

It does not matter how much he charms, seduces, manipulates, or lies to his supply source, his toxic nature will always show itself. The vampire will eventually display its contempt for all humankind. All communication with the monster is a competition however only he knows that he is competing. Those who are unfortunate enough to feel love, compassion, or empathy for him will be consumed and eventually discarded. The vampire preys upon those who are willing to allow its feeding frenzy. A narcissist smells empathy like a Hollywood created vampire smells blood. Although he is incapable of empathy on his own, he is cunning enough to sniff it out in his victims and use it as a tool for manipulation, power, and control.

Narcissists generally present as overbearing bullies or shy victims however there is often a spectrum to their presentation. They have quite a performance range and they love to blame others for their situation. This seems to be a constant. Never underestimate narcissists for these monsters possess cunning and pathological survival abilities. Skills that will drain the vitality out of their victim's lives and make it seem like the victims want their life controlled and destroyed. They are very adept at presenting situations they manipulate in such a way as to infer that it is the victims fault for the situation. Lacking empathy and/or compassion is a sure, recognizable sign of both overt and covert narcissists. Another obvious red flag is their openly displayed and(sometimes) secret delusions of grandeur. Their disdain for "mere mortals" becomes obvious with detached observation. While I believe that many narcissists harbor an innate sense of worthlessness, I do not think this is the case for all narcissists. I believe some narcissists are convinced of the validity of their own bogus superpowers. Both covert and overt narcissists display an observable drive to accomplish the compulsive, pathological, exploitation, manipulation, and resource acquisition of their victims. Their obvious need to denigrate others both psychologically and sometimes even physically is observable and undeniable. Both Overt and Covert narcissists use denial, dishonesty, shaming language, gas lighting, flying monkeys, blame, Triangulation, Love Bombing, and psychological punishment to serve their selfish ends. As much as they love to extol their toxic opinions, they are natural masters of the "silent treatment."

While abusive vampires are almost all observable toxic energy leeches, and they can quickly smother your life in drama don't lose hope. You can use their common, observable tactics and behaviors as new tools for freedom. Awareness breeds movement. When observing an abuser it is easy to suffer from "Paralysis of analysis." Their nasty behavior patterns may be more or less obvious depending upon their levels of hunger and survival needs. Here are some of the more obvious signs, behaviors, and patterns that you can observe to help you recognize, avoid, and contain the damage by both overt and covert Vampires/Narcissists.

Traits of the Vampire

1. The Vampire/Narcissist is not truly human in my opinion. A human can control his base instincts, but an animal cannot. In contrast to a human, the animal is led and controlled by instincts. The narcissist lacks empathy and

compassion because he (or she) is an instinct driven animal in human form. This monster can only mimic compassion and empathy. The faster you understand this the safer you will become. The vampire is incapable of caring for anyone. It always lacks empathy for the people it uses. Humans in general are just tools for its use. It may attempt to fake empathy or victimhood sometimes. This is just an attempt to feed on the victim's energy, both positive and negative. The vampire will not be convincing in the long term if properly observed. It will always be convinced that it is believable because the vampire always believes his own dysfunctional, instinct driven internal narrative. This is a given because the vampire's fragile ego is always locked into his position. If his position falls, his ego falls with it. The vampire will always protect his ego and never willingly allow his position to fall. He will exhibit an obvious grandiose affect co-occurring with a toxic lack of awareness of, or concern for, the feelings and needs of other people. He will obviously care nothing for the opinion of others except when the opinion can advance his cause and increase or insure his supply. Once he has no use for his supply he will discard his supply. He will not discard without another supply firmly locked down. The narcissist always "Monkey-branches" meaning that he/she/it only let's go of one supply source when another source is firmly within its grasp.

2. The creature will eventually display and reveal its toxic delusions of grandeur. The vampire will attack psychologically and even physically if its delusions are threatened in any way. There will always be chaos attached to interaction with the vampire. This chaos will be ongoing, creating toxic drama in any life the narcopath shares with an actual human.

3. It is a guarantee that he (or she) will intentionally, ruthlessly, and relentlessly manipulate people, places, and things to obtain and ensure the chosen supply source. The narcissist will go to extreme measures to ensure that the supply continues uninterrupted. That is a given until the vampire locates another supply source it feels is better and more abundant in energy and resources.

4. The vampire/narcissist cannot and will not accept any form of criticism willingly. Criticism is simply not allowed, nor is truthful observation. Constructive criticism or even positive feedback that does not fit his demented narrative will be a good enough reason for him to attack. He will not and cannot ever allow challenges to his perceived status to remain unanswered.

He will lash out overtly or use covert, societal violence against anyone who questions his delusional position. His communication method is always win-lose communication. The vampire must always win for he is always "right." He will always seek revenge just for the sake of harming a former supply source. The vampire will discard its supply eventually for the creature's pathology is always destructive. It is always hunting for more energy and resources to supply its unbalanced cravings. The leech will always monkey branch from one energy source to another source. Please remember that the vampire will not let go of a supply source until it has secured another supply source. The narcopaths grip is the firm grip of the insane. Remember this fact.

5. The vampire will never make a genuine apology. The narcopath will never take actual responsibility for its toxic manipulations. Accountability is unknown to him/her.

6. If the disturbed monster's mouth is moving, the leech is lying.

7. The vampire will always rationalize its actions, words and current situation by blaming other people and circumstances for his deeds, words, or consequences for his actions. The narcissist

sees people, places, and things as tools to be used to obtain energy and supply. There is no exception to this fact.

8.   He will manipulate, attack, persecute, mislead, lie, and psychologically punish anyone who opposes his instinct driven desires. He will denigrate and attempt to eliminate anyone who seeks to deprive him of control over his supply. The vampire is literally capable of any manipulation in order to advance his demented "cause."

9.   The vampire will observably use a divide and conquer strategy to gain the support and cooperation of his allies. (Triangulation and flying monkeys are the vampires favorite tools.) These tools may often include the family members, friends, acquaintances, and co-workers of his chosen supply source.

10. Manipulation and control are always his obvious goals. His language and communication methods may contain obscenities and often are riddled with observable logical fallacies, especially Straw Man, Ad Hominin, False Dichotomy, False Premise, Circular Reasoning, and closed ended questions.

Overt Vampire Tactics

1. He is driven with an uncontrollable instinct to attract attention to himself always. He is toxic and compulsive in his desire to be noticed by anyone and everyone. He is equally content with positive or negative attention as all attention is used to feed his unfillable ego.

2. This brand of toxic vampire often perceives itself as an "Alpha Male or Alpha Female" and demands admiration and agreement from all people encountered. In the absence of his supply, (in the form of agreement) it will react with observable impatience and sometimes even rage to display his self-perceived superiority for all to see. He assumes that everyone operates out of fear-based thinking as he does. He is angered and surprised when he cannot elicit fear, awe, and automatic deference and respect from someone.

3. He views other people as his servants. He acts as if he is superior to others. He is an "Expert without a portfolio." His opinion is the only opinion he ever considers, and this is one of his most observable weaknesses, not a strength. The time bandit is a self-proclaimed "expert" in all fields. This is especially true if he is accomplished in a specific field of endeavor. However unrelated his field is from the topic

being discussed he will have a strong opinion to communicate to all present.

4.   He gives in to a toxic and compulsive anger at will. Anger is his favorite fuel. Anger is instinctive for the narcopath. It is his "Go to" answer for any encounter that does not validate his opinion or position. The vampire cannot regulate his base emotions reliably and it is wise to remember that he is never influenced by compassion. He is in a constant internal struggle to win at all costs and everything is a contest. He sometimes displays a rage that exceeds a normal anger response. This is because his rage stems from a vampire's instinctual desperation coupled with the toxic hunger of a predator. He must maintain his ego/position at all costs because one supports the other. He feels justified in using physical violence when he sees fit to use physical violence. Only his opinion on when to use violence matters. He will engage in societal violence to obtain his manipulative goals. He feeds on relational violence. The vampire loves twitter campaigns, trolling on Facebook, starting rumors at work, filing false reports, costing people their jobs, and an atmosphere of chaos in general. The vampire will do anything to harm his perceived "enemy's." Once he discards his supply he will

usually try to destroy or humiliate his former energy source by any means necessary.

5. He sees other people as pawns to be used and sacrificed, or as competitors to be defeated and humiliated. He wants to win at all costs and he feels that he always deserves to win.

6. His "rapier like wit" always involves ridiculing others. He observably enjoys denigrating people in a toxic game of one-upmanship. Only he knows the game is even being played however. He may pretend he is "Just joking" and resort to gas lighting to confuse and manipulate his targets. He can mimic emotions he does not actually feel.

7. He obviously expects that he deserves special treatment and he demands special treatment. He displays entitlement in his words, deeds, and actions. These observable traits are most visible when the narcissist interacts with wait staff and service personnel. The narcissist's behavior at hotels and restaurants are especially revealing of his toxic, unpleasant nature. Depending on his motives he can be charming and suave, however he is dangerous and manipulative always. His humor is almost always at the expense of others. Denial is his art form.

Covert Vampire Tactics

1. Permanent victim status coupled with passive-aggressive manipulation is the pattern to observe for when detecting a covert narcissist. To get her/his way this vampire will play the victim convincingly. These particular vampires are very adept at gaining the trust of people in authority. People like police, medical staff, counselors, therapists, judges, etc. They may become particularly dangerous if put in check via saving their toxic communication with documentation. While possibly dangerous, they are also vulnerable to documentation in the form of recorded outbursts, texts, e-mails, phone messages, etc. Documenting their toxic and dangerous behavior must be attempted in the quest for freedom. It is wise to be careful and precise for they are very good at "Flipping the script." They are often helpless when properly documented, reported, and held accountable.

2. The covert narcissist is observably smug, obviously insensitive, and often uses sex and intimacy as a weapon (Just like the overt vampire.) This vampire withholds and dispenses attention and affection to control and manipulate his supply source. Do not look for empathy or understanding for there is none to be found. You cannot "fix" this brand of crazy.

This particular minion of chaos does not want to be fixed because they assume they are perfect.

3.   This monster especially likes to exploit people who are kind, caring, considerate, and who think they can "help," fix," or "heal" the poor, broken victim/vampire. Much like a great white shark, these monsters seem to be able to detect one-part empathy in a million parts of any environment.

4.   This monster can often emote on demand. Their ability to mimic emotion makes them especially deceptive and cunning. They can cry on cue and manipulate the unwary with energetic, and emotional academy award level performances. This makes them particularly dangerous due to being convincing. The covert vampire uses the same logical fallacies as the overt, as well as the closed ended statements and questions. Most notable narcissistic communication fallacies are the personal Attack, False Premise/Assumed Premise, False Dichotomy, Circular Reasoning, and Straw Man arguments.

5.   This vampire observably displays delusions of grandeur co-occurring with tales of victimization, abuse, and persecution. This vampire plays the blame game at a championship level. It loves to blame others and insist "It's not my fault." Please remember:

6. **The Narcissists motto is "I did not do that."**

7. **The Narcissists slogan is "It's never my fault, it's your fault I did that." (But I still didn't do it.)**

8. **The Narcissists oath is "You asked for it, that's why I did it." ("But I still didn't do it and you're crazy for accusing me."**

9. The toxic vampire/narcissist loves and craves relational drama with an intensity that demonstrates his true insanity. The vampire will create a real or fake crisis to gain attention and drain energy (for his consumption) from his supply and secondary supply. Triangulation via monkey branching will be used during the discard phase of the vampire's current supply source.

10. This monster loves to create a crisis and then react (and manipulate others to react) to the self-created crisis. The monster has no qualms exaggerating suffering and sickness to gain support and sympathy for the self-created cause. They are driven pathologically/instinctually to custom create "causes" that result in drama, pain, and discord for all involved. All manipulation is good manipulation for the vampire. The same is true of energy. Positive and negative energy is equally fulfilling for the vampire.

11. They usually have a history of drug abuse and addiction, usually co-occurring with (self-proclaimed) PTSD, depression and anxiety. They may also have a criminal record. They will claim that none of this is their fault.

12. The vampire will always be a drain on their current supply source (partner/family) of precious time, energy, money and resources. This is the true nature of this particular beast and it is a pattern worth noting.

13. There is always someone other than themselves to blame for their self-created challenges, problems, shortcomings, crises, and failures. The blame is always placed on "unfair" people, places, things, and circumstances. The vampire always claims he is blameless and a self-proclaimed victim.

14. The vampire will never change on his own. He will only change his feeding habits and sources, never his twisted dynamic. Like the mythical vampire his patterns are the result of a pathology that is incurable.

Chapter Seven

Make an escape plan

CREATE AN ESCAPE PLAN (but be willing to adapt to evolving situations.)

Once you recognize the vampire for the dangerous, abusive monster he is you need an exit plan. You may feel trapped and overwhelmed due to children in the relationship. Even if you have children together you need an exit plan. Especially if you have children with the abuser. This is a priority because the children are learning the ways of the narcopath. They are being conditioned to experience the toxic narcissistic relationship as "normal." Narcissism is an evil gift that keeps on giving. It is the ultimate "Mind Virus." The narcissist can and will exploit children. The narcissist is incapable of empathy and children are just tools to be used by him for his toxic agenda. A narcissist cannot control his toxic, instinct driven pathology. This compassionless dynamic will harm children for life. They will become used to living with a minion of chaos. The chaos driven environment will harm them. Get out quickly. If you have no children with the narcissist keep it that way. Do so for your own good and the good of your unborn children.

Start to think about how you are going to leave the vampire behind for your own rational self-interest. You deserve healthy interactions and relationships. Think about how you will relocate. Start to consider where exactly you're going relocate to, and who might be able to assist you in escaping. You must be discrete and cover your preparations well. Staying low-key about your preperations will help you maintain safety and hopefully avoid drama and chaos. In the Army I learned a mantra: "Fail to plan, Plan to fail." Preparing to leave your home is a difficult undertaking. It is not impossible. You did not come to reside there in a flash so don't think you can just leave in a flash. Make careful preparations if possible. If you think you might have to leave the home quickly then you will most likely need immediate help. Do not be afraid to ask for support. Allies are everywhere you just don't know them yet. Leaving the abuser bestows upon you rewards that you may not recognize currently. Rewards that staying with the abuser will prevent you from ever knowing. After the psychological pain subsides (and it will) you will realize some awesome moments of clarity. You will be able to see the nightmare relationship for what it actually is and not the dream you wanted it to be. When you live in the present you will regain your self-respect. When you are thankful for the lessons you have embraced healing.

Being accountable for resolving your challenges:

I am influenced strongly from the substance abuse model of recovery. My clients start with an assessment. Then they create a recovery plan that addresses their recovery goals. The plan has goals, methods, and interventions. Producing healthy and positive recovery outcomes requires planning. You are entering recovery. You are recovering and reclaiming your life back from an abusive predator. To do this, you need to recognize and claim your own accountability within this dynamic. I see the value in accountability every day. I am going to challenge you to be accountable for your challenges in relationship. Let's begin with a simple recovery safety plan, the first step to creating a recovery/treatment plan. I want you to be accountable and custom design a recovery safety plan just for you. A plan that will help you attain freedom from abuse and dysfunction. Let's consider what to put in the plan. Use these suggestions as a brain storm. I keep things to the number three so that my clients are not overwhelmed. You may face many challenges right now but addressing three is do-able. You can always address more as you finish with the original three challenges. Be kind to yourself and resist the urge to take on more than you can handle. Set yourself up for success, not failure.

What three changes do you want to make regarding your current relationship?

Name three reasons why you desire these changes.

Name three steps you plan to take in changing the current relationship

Select three safe people you can go to for support in making these changes.

Name three ways you will know that your changes are effective.

Name three challenges that could derail your plans for healthy change.

What three things will you do to stay accountable to your safety plan?

List three people you can call that will help you maintain accountability during your transition.

List three people in your support network.

What I am trying to help you realize is that accountability on your part is the most important ingredient in producing your successful outcomes. If possible, try to enroll an accountability partner into your efforts at healthy change. Find someone who will help you stay focused and help you through moments of weakness. We all have those moments. In recovery we call these people sponsors. Abusive relationships have a way of becoming embedded within our lives. They can become repetitive. It takes discipline, and accountability to make and sustain lasting change. Even if you must use an online support forum under a secure account then make that happen. It is not ideal, but it is better than nothing at all. Some forums are awesome. I belong to several narcissistic abuse recovery groups on social media.

It really helps to share the load with someone else when you are transitioning to wholeness. Leaving a toxic relationship is challenging but not hopeless. Be very upfront and honest with your accountability partner. Let them know clearly what you need from them. Talk with them about accountability. Find out their views on the subject. Look for inspiration, honesty, and communication. Select someone willing to engage you honestly and give you solid, constructive feedback. You do not need another person in your life who is trying to control you, use you, or manipulate you. Do not give away your power. You know they are a good accountability partner if they call you on your lack of boundaries. Online forums are a great place to process your challenges and lessons learned both pre and post Narcopath. They are also useful places to practice your boundary setting skills. You can practice being assertive and not aggressive. This decision to have an accountability partner is a crucial one. You may not know the red flags to look for. You may need practice, so don't be afraid to try out many different accountability partners if you need to do so. Don't be afraid to practice in online forums first. Forums have rules and guidelines. Your boundaries are important. Please remember that honest feedback may be difficult to accept. Your best accountability partner may not be the easiest to accept feedback from. Honesty is key. Yours and theirs.

Things to talk about: Your goals and their timely implementation. Ideas on rational self-interest. Your feelings regarding love bombing, hoovering, triangulation, flying monkeys, and self-limiting thoughts and beliefs. Boundary setting and how to communicate your needs. Any triggers that cause you to want to continue the toxic dynamic. Make sure your accountability partner is someone who you can count on to be discreet.

Plan, prepare, protect yourself, and leave.

Technology is wonderful. If it is not illegal to do so, record the idiot's rampages and diatribes on a cellphone or electronic device without his knowledge. You can then upload these toxic scenes to the cloud where he cannot obtain them. You can secretly and carefully position the phone, so he cannot see it, (on a bookshelf for example.) Save the videos to files and e-mail the files to trusted friends and/or relatives. Once you are safe, (and only if it is legal) you might start a you-tube or patrion channel and post his toxic stupidity for all to see. An old African saying is that "It takes a village to raise a child." I say, "It takes a village to expose a narcopath." If you have pictures, police reports, and video of the physical abuse remember to take it all with you when you finally leave. Don't leave files on a shared computer. E-mail those files to a secret e-mail address only you know about for collection later. Do everything twice and even three times so you have backup evidence. Erase your history trail. Assume he will snoop on the computer even if it is not his computer. Take screenshots of his posts and store all abusive e-mails. You can also print them and keep them in a secret physical file he cannot access. Keep your phone and mobile devices locked down so the idiot cannot prowl upon them. Keep a secret phone if possible. Remove or destroy the hard drive before you leave. Leave him nothing that he can use to hurt you with later. Whatever he can use to smear you or harm you with, he will. The minion of chaos loves manipulation. Make sure that it is impossible for the abuser to ever discover your evidence of his or her abuse. If they ever find it the narcissist will attempt to destroy it or "flip the script" with law enforcement. You can be sure of this, because this is one of the patterns of the monster.

If you can do so safely, send files and paper copies to a close, reliable friend or a trusted family member. If you can safely expose the creature, then by all means do so. Always have backups. Never allow (if possible) the abusive vampire to even know or suspect any evidence exists. This might increase your risk for more volatile, unsafe, and violent actions from the narcissist/vampire. Pictures or video evidence from phones and electronic devices might include: *Anything with a date on it. Hospital reports can be quickly recorded via snapshot applications on phones, as can police reports. All injuries should be documented even if you do not go to a hospital. Voice recordings of rants, threats, and hateful diatribes are a plus. Pictures of bruises, cuts, scrapes, wrecked clothing, blood stains, and hair pulled out are all powerful and compelling evidence. It is easy to obtain small, discrete hidden video recorders now due to advances in technology. Use them but be careful, legal, and discrete. Narcissists and abusers can be dangerous when exposed. They never back down unless forced to back down. If he broke windows, doors, family pictures, vases, furniture or punched holes in walls during a toxic diatribe, take pictures when it is safe to do so. Do not antagonize the toxic vampire during an abusive, dangerous outburst. Get to safety first, record with discretion in mind always. Your physical well-being is primary. Video or pictures that show the destruction can be powerful tools for you to use if you choose to use those tools.*

Try your best to record and document everything the vampire does that is even remotely dangerous, obviously crazy, criminal, or just plain stupid. This may be important for you later. If he lies online, screenshot and print. If he makes crazy threats or claims that are easily refuted, screenshot and print. If he sends ridiculous, threatening e-mails and texts, save them, print them, place them in secret physical files. Make this a habit and make sure people read them, even if you must post them online. Online support groups can be invaluable but be advised that narcs love to stalk online. They often join support groups looking for victims. They also like to pose as "experts" and "help" victims of narcissistic abuse. Sometimes they just troll to get reactions and feed on negative energy. Your safety and life are worth fighting for but fight smart. Refuse to allow the vampire to dictate the terms of your life anymore. You must fight back but fight with a calm and sober purpose. Narcissists/vampires need more light and less heat, light exposes and destroys them. Light drains their perceived power.

Let's review the important things to record, photograph, video, etc.:

Any images of his destructive acts, holes in walls, broken dinnerware, or smashed furniture or personal property. All records of you being treated for injuries caused by the idiot. All police reports that had to be made due to his stupidity, cruelty, or criminal acts. Anything that will prove to people what an abusive imbecile he is in real life. Please tell people when he hurts you or scares you. If you are injured get treatment at the nearest emergency room. Remember to tell everyone you speak too in the medical setting what the vampire did to you. Give them an accurate chronology of events and when they release you from treatment get a copy of your records. Make sure the idiot cannot access them. Use your phone to record all abusive events and injuries. Although journals can be dangerous I think they can also be very helpful and useful if employed with a sense of safety. The only real danger to a journal is if the abusive narcopath finds the journal. Other than that, journals can be both therapeutic and healing. They can provide you with powerful self-insight later. Especially if you are trauma bonded to your narcissist and have self-doubts after leaving the abusive situation. Journal the vampire idiot's rantings, threats, and abuse, both verbal and physical. Remember to date the entries because these dates will line up with phone messages, texts, photos, e-mails, and other records that you keep that will show the truth. These ideas are just me brainstorming, everyone's situation varies. However the one constant is that all vampires/narcissists have some observable commonalities. You should brainstorm also because you can do it silently if you have to. Abusers will say and do abusive, stupid, and destructive things and they will display their dysfunction. You must catch their unbalanced, destructive, patterns in such a way that you can prove their dangerous, abusive pathology and relational stupidity in court.

Narcissists love to be "Right" and they love to "prove" everyone else "wrong." One of their weaknesses that you can exploit is their penchant for occasionally sending abusive and threatening diatribes, e-mails, voicemails, and text messages. I cannot emphasize this enough. This is important. Please keep these in a file both electronic and physical that the narcissist cannot access. Save them because they will come in handy later. It is a good idea to have a "ready bag" in a safe place where the narcissist cannot ever find it. I know this is touchy but please do your best. Make sure to have some essentials in your ready bag. Essentials include: Your ID, passport, driver's license, State ID card, etc. Car keys that the idiot knows nothing about may be essential. When you obtain spares without his knowledge be discrete. Right before you leave it is a good idea to destroy all joint credit cards. Make sure you cancel them and keep a list of them, so you can review their history later. The narcissist may use fraud and deceit to have them re-issued for his use. Keep your personal credit cards but be aware that the dysfunctional monster is capable of anything. Keep your checkbook and make sure to close old accounts and open a new account at a different bank or branch before or after you leave. If you can open a new bank account before you leave so much the better. Just make sure it is a different bank or credit union altogether. Bank at a branch nowhere near where the idiot lives. If you can stash money away before you leave, then great! Do it. Take any money that is yours and do not feel guilty. You are escaping a monster who does not possess empathy. Make sure you have any medications you or your children need as well as refill information. After you leave, the narcissist will go to great lengths to try and destroy you. This may include interfering with medication for both you and the children. Be prepared for the actual animal to show his true colors. Humans can control their instincts, animals are led by their instincts. The narcissist is an animal in human form. Never forget this fact. Make sure you have clothes for yourself and your children. Once you leave he will try to make your life a living hell and that includes hurting you by any means necessary. Abusers love making it impossible to pick up anything from your former home after you leave. What he does not destroy, he will use as a lever for manipulation. Video the rooms before you leave and include a date/time stamp if possible. If you must, buy a newspaper and include that in the photograph to prove the date. Narcissists are known to destroy and damage property and blame their victim.

Make sure that keepsakes and deeply personal items are kept safe. Things like family heirlooms, jewelry, clothing, toys, etc. are priorities to take with you. This may take extra planning, but it is worth it. The narcopath will destroy or use as a tool for control anything important that you leave behind. You do not want to give the narcissist any weapons to use against you. Plan to store these items with close friends or family members far in advance. If possible, rent a small, discrete, storage locker that the narcopath knows nothing about. Make sure you have contact information for supportive and loyal friends, and family members. Also have numbers for Uber, Lyft, bus service information, taxis, school information, and outside support group information. Learn the locations of places that may be useful such as domestic violence shelter information. I cannot emphasize enough that it is important to not forget birth certificates, school records, transcripts, court orders, protection orders, social security cards, shot records, passports, and personal photographs. These items will be denied to you (or destroyed) if the narcopath is left with them. You will then face the daunting task of applying for these records all over again. If you do not properly prepare, your exit plan will be a bumpy ride. However your life comes first. If you must leave quickly to stay safe, then leave immediately. Death is permanent, records can be gained again.

Hide your ready bag where the narcopath will never find it. Remember that the narcissist is a master of defamation, deceit, manipulation, and character assassination. He can and will convince people that he is the victim. You must use discernment in selecting which friends or family members to hide your belongings with. The narcissist will pathologically corrupt relationships. The vampire will recruit allies and his "Flying Monkeys" are strangely loyal. Flying monkeys have a toxic dedication only deceived people seem to display. The narcissist will know to look into your close friends and family. He will know your online social platform notifications better than you do. Forget neighbors who live close by your home and forget any mutual friends. The narcissist has most likely been feeding them mis-information and lies all along. You really have no idea how the narcissist has already manipulated them. Now, in the preparation phase of leaving, you must make some monumental survival decisions. Who do you trust? Depending on how deep the narcissist has infiltrated your life you may face this transition alone. It may be better to have a secret storage locker. If you do have a supportive friend or family member, remember to have them be discrete also. It will not serve your higher good to have them accidentally say the wrong words to a mutual friend who then reports what was said to the narcopath.

Do your best to stash some money for yourself. Narcissists tend to be manipulative and controlling with money. They use money as a tool and a method of oversight. They usually do not want their food/energy source to possess money. This may be the biggest challenge you face. The narcissist usually wants their victim to be under their financial thumb. This usually translates into "they make all financial decisions." Narcopaths love to control all the money and keep their victim dependent upon them. They are very skilled at financial control. They can destroy their victims financially even when they make no money and add nothing to the "relationship."

Try to find out about free or low cost vocational training near you that you can take advantage of in order to prepare you for a job when you leave. It is best to escape from the vampire when he cannot be around to stop you. If he is violent, call police, press charges, and file a restraining order. Many domestic violence shelters will help you with this. Start putting up boundaries between you and the abuser/narcissist. Begin setting limits. If he is in jail, make sure you are gone when he gets out. Narcissists cannot be "wrong" and if proven so they will go into championship level denial about the facts concerning their "victimhood." Remember, the vampire's ego is so connected to its position that if whatever position they are attached to falls, their ego collapses with it. I cannot emphasize this fact enough. If the narcopaths position faces threats due to logic, reason, or interference from authorities, they will go to extreme lengths to be "right." Their ego must never be allowed to fall because this will wreck them. The narcissist will prop up his defenses and dig in deeply to "win" even if it destroys someone. They sometimes destroy themselves by this pathology.

Narcissists are natural stalkers by nature. They are attracted to people who will allow their predations. Having no empathy or compassion, they can focus their manipulations like a laser beam. They probe weaknesses and take advantage of emotions in their prey. Many people find that a narcissist from their past will look them up after years of no contact. These creatures assume that they can win any challenge and their past actions do not matter to them. Narcissists hunt constantly for supply, new and old. Energy is their fuel, especially financial energy. When you leave, contact the three credit bureaus and have fraud alerts put on your credit reports. Ask your credit card companies to report any unusual activity on your card. Remember that social media is a narcissists favorite hunting ground. They can and will try to track you through social media postings. They will even go so far as to create false accounts in order to join groups you are in on social media. Online stalking is a reality and the narcissist will not hesitate to use his flying monkeys to triangulate you. If he has ever had access to your social security card, contact social security right away and let people know that you are in danger of someone using your number. They can print you a report. If you exercise, use a gym, or go to classes, do so with other people present. Never be alone where the narcissist can confront, stalk, manipulate, and make things up. They will create drama and chaos if they can possibly do so. Remember to always look for security cameras when you are in stores. Try to be aware of their locations so you can be under them in case the narcissist suddenly shows up where you are and confronts you. Avoid arguing with him, just dial 911, talk to the dispatcher, and wait under the camera for help to arrive.

You have some great defensive weapons at your disposal right away. A cell phone, going no contact, and your feelings/instincts. Keep important numbers programmed into your phone for instant access. Trusted friends, shelters, police and emergency numbers are a few you may want to have programed in ahead of time. If you feel nervous or unsafe don't ignore these promptings. Find a safe space to regain your bearings. Make sure you create a safe network of people that you can call. If you are in a mall and your narcissist shows up, calmly walk to the mall security area quickly or to the nearest mall security officer. Do not argue or fight with the narcissist. Speak calmly and clearly to the mall security officer as well as the police dispatcher. Video the narcissist with your phone. Stay calm and communicate clearly with authorities.

Build a custom support network for yourself. Find and attend outside support groups. Recovery groups like Al-anon, or groups for battered women or narcissistic support groups are good starts. Network with people who have experienced similar challenges and struggles. Communicate with other survivors, people who have dealt with abuse in general and a narcissist in particular. If you do run into the vampire by accident, lead him into the light. Do not go to your new address. Go instead to a police station, a battered women's shelter, or a random gym and pay the day fee to mislead him. Do anything but allow him access into your new, "No contact" life. Call your friends that he does not know and have them meet you in a coffee shop you never go to. Do not lead the vampire near your home or the homes of your new friends if you can help it. Your safety comes first and remember my motto: "It takes a village to expose a narcopath."

Chapter Seven affirmations:

I allow and attract healthy people into my life.

I recognize toxic people and I avoid them effortlessly.

I deserve a calm, healthy life.

I make my own survival decisions.

Chapter Eight

Rebuilding your life

Your narcissist most likely impeded your independence in many ways. Work is important to healthy human beings. Rewarding work not only helps us provide for ourselves, the right kind of work also provides us with a purpose. A job we like and enjoy doing is one of the best and strongest tools in your post narcissist survival tool chest. It is a strong part of taking back your power and recreating yourself. Finding purpose in your life is the ultimate "do-over." Humans are social creatures and interacting with other people on the job can be rewarding and fun. All work places have their challenges, but they also have their own unique culture. Exploring and becoming part of that culture, along with having meaningful work, helps you to feel a sense of belonging. Many people who work together become friends and socialize together. This makes sense when you realize that shared work and workplace experiences often help people to create, build, and cement a common bond with each other. This can be humanity at its best.

Consider the positive possibilities of work.

After years as food for an energy leech your self-esteem engine has been running on fumes. Finding work will help you fill your self-esteem tank. This is especially true if the vampire in your past life forbid you to work and controlled all the money. Most narcissists are very insecure about their supply becoming independent. It is hard to feel strong and independent when you are constantly put down. Abusers fear strong people.

The past is dead; you are not your past. The future has not yet happened. You have only the present moment, moment to moment, and your choices within each moment will become your future. Seeing this process can begin growth in a new direction.

You will feel conflict about old "friends" who still support the narcissist. However, if you examine the dynamic clearly you will see that these "friendships" were really centered upon the minion of chaos. Narcissistic abuse can sometimes involve co-dependency, trauma bonding, possible drug use, manipulation and even a criminal lifestyle. The destructive interactions were based upon non–stop thinking errors and self-centered, ego driven motives rooted within the culture of toxic narcissism. These mutual "friends" exist because the narcissist must always be in control and "right." Everyone else is always "wrong," especially you. These "friends" who help the narcissist are called "Flying monkeys" for good reason. The narcissist will always try to manipulate and use others as a lever to force you into their "approved" way of thinking. Consider this question for a minute, *why do they need to help the narcissist?* If they were real friends and thus fair and unbiased why would they support the vampire and "observe and report" for his (or her) benefit? These misled and manipulated "friends" will expect you to obey the narcissist and crave his approval as they do. They mean nothing to the narcissist. Their efforts on his behalf can only benefit the narcissists self -centered, ego driven, twisted world view. There is nothing noble or intelligent about being used as a tool for an emotionally stunted, selfish, forever adolescent, perpetual energy leech. Especially one who is constantly making stupid decisions. Interacting with flying monkeys is just like interacting with the narcissist as it only leads to chaos, drama, the involvement of social services, courts, and possibly law enforcement. It also leads to a life diverted from its true purpose. Your life interrupted. Grey rock or go no contact with these "friends" just as you would the narcissist. You will be thankful for it later.

A survivor does not expect others to make her survival choices. *Why would you allow toxic ego driven, narcissistic, dysfunctional, dangerous, immature people to make your survival decisions?* If they cared about you at all they would withhold judgement, never take sides, encourage your new growth and never want you to suffer mental or physical abuse. They would listen to you and pay attention. Flying monkeys are never your "friends." These kind of "friends" will endanger your mental health, and possibly your freedom. Eventually they will knowingly or unknowingly assist the narcissist in crushing your dreams. They desire and need approval from the narcissist just as you once craved and needed his approval. They are just as trapped within the narcissist's web of deceit and manipulation as you once were. They will be discarded once they are of no use to the vampire. They just want some dysfunctional company as they swim within the cesspool of the narcissist. They want to stay within their comfort zone as food for a vampire. They have accepted their role as narcissistic supply. They want someone to share lies with as they live in denial, ruled by their ego as well as the narcissist's ego. Living their drama filled life on the installment plan created by the narcissist. Being drained daily by the vampire is their choice, not yours anymore. *You are not your past choices, but you will become your present choices.*

A new job can help you distance yourself from old "friends" and outdated habits invalidated by your new growth post narcissist. When approached by old friends and associates who "Observe and report" for the vampire you can always blame your heavy work load. Just don't let them know where you work or what your compensation is. Be vague and unclear about where you work. Tell them you are taking classes. Use misdirection and be boring about it. I am suggesting that it is ok to lie to flying monkeys. Lie if you must to divert the narcissist, but I think silence or re-direction is the best policy. Think like a survivor. If "mutual friends" run into you randomly, simply say you are on your way to an appointment. You are under no obligation to tell them anything. Change the topic, ask them how they are doing, and deflect the conversation back on them. Flying Monkeys will always observe and report back to the narcissist. I recommend that you work overtime if possible as you adjust to life post narcissist. Work two jobs if you can. These pro-active decisions on your part will take a huge bite out of the possible time that flying monkeys and the vampire have available to them. Time they would squander in order to snoop and pry into your affairs. Be as unavailable and as invisible as a grey rock on a rock-strewn beach. Remember, your goal is to heal. In the process of healing you will gain back your life, take back your control, avoid unnecessary drama, and accomplish a vampire free life. The work, both paid and volunteer, along with classes and hobbies will fill your life with purpose. Your personal empowerment will come from insight and growth.

Choices are everywhere, and choices impact the future as well as the present.

You can use the world of work as well as your class schedule to shield you from both flying monkeys and triangulation. Narcopath driven challenges will come your way. Staying busy is the key to your continued freedom and happiness. Post vampire is your time to re-connect with life. You were not free with the narcissist. You will not stay free if you allow flying monkeys to invade your space. Give the flying monkeys no information. Just go to work, school, or training and be intense about it. Fill your life with new experiences. If every time the vampire tries to check up on you he or she finds nothing that feeds him with positive or negative energy, he will starve. Your goal is to eventually become boring. *Boring is GOOD post narcissist.* The narcissist has a huge, unfillable void and he or she is hungry for energy. Their appetite for drama will eventually need their full effort and attention. This is especially true if you left the narcissist pre-discard. If you prove over time that you are as boring and uninteresting as a grey rock, your old, outdated narcissist will move on to more exciting people. People who will accept becoming his supply source. People who will fill the role he demands. There are only twenty-four hours in a day. You must eat, sleep, work, take care of household chores, and pay bills. The more you fill these hours with work and positive endeavors the safer you are post narcissist. Just remember to stay in the "light" because vampires hate sunlight. Become that boring person to your narcissist by starving him of any attention both positive and negative. You simply will not have a lot of time available to become drawn into the negative situations and custom created drama caused by flying monkeys. These idiots love the darkness of destructive triangulations and manufactured dysfunction. They are always eager to report back to their master. Allow them to dwell within their chosen darkness alone.

Your choices within the present moment become your future.

The narcissist's goal is to always know where you are and what you are doing. The vampire stalks you so he can manipulate situations to his advantage. He is always hungry. When you make work, training, or school a survival tactic, you will have no time for the vampire and he will starve. Your former "friends" still supporting the old narcissistic lifestyle will move on to other victims at the behest of the narcissist. The members of the dark clown circus will play their dysfunctional games without you. This is wonderful even if you don't know it yet. Eventually your old Vampire will find another victim because they are pathologically committed to feeding upon other people's energy and resources. Some narcopaths will die of overdoses (almost always unintentional.) Some will die due to violence. Some will get locked up in steel cages where they belong. Most will live out their lives in drama, conflict, and misery. Unfortunately, they will make anyone living with them suffer right along with them. Their dysfunctional, unhealthy lifestyle choices will take them away from you eventually. By creating and following your current healthy thoughts, you will find freedom from the narcissist. You have the power to change the old dynamic. By following your past unhealthy thoughts, you were captured by the vampire. Remember that reality and don't repeat it.

Thinking eventually creates situations, and situations impact your life for the better or worse.

When you were with the vampire you were manipulated into a controlled lifestyle that became unbearable. If you were able to obtain one of the soul crushing, sometimes nasty jobs that the vampire approved of, you most likely hated it. Along with financial control you were subjected to drama, insults, and bulling by the narcopath. Even if you must take a minimum wage job after leaving your narcissist just know it is a beginning and not an end. It is your job and your money. You are starting your life again. You have the power to choose your attitude about the situation. Always remember that you are still recreating yourself. You are a being becoming someone new. No one owes you anything, and you are entitled to nothing except that which you earn on your own merits. Society in general and life in particular will constantly be in process of *demanding things of you*. You are in no position to demand anything from life, no one is in that position. *Now is your time to deliver and prove yourself*, so see this as an opportunity to meet the challenges of life. In doing so, you will create a new, more positive existence for yourself. You have more freedom now than you had with the narcissist. Within freedom lies opportunity. Remember also that you will learn new skills, adapt, and also improve on a healthy continuum. Your first survival job will not be your last job, just a step along a new path.

The narcissist mentality has reinforced the victim and the predator roles simultaneously. Narcissists think that they can demand things from life. They assume that they are automatically entitled to resources, attention, praise, and another's energy. Healthy people know that life demands things from us, and we are entitled to nothing except what we earn. Strength to mentally healthy people is the ability to respond well to the demands of life. The entitlement mentality, the victim mentality, the predator mentality, these are perceived as an unbalanced life. These are seen as a sign of weakness by society. Unfortunately, the victims of these vampires are perceived as weak and defective people also. Society admires people who lead creative, organized lives. People who are efficient and responsible with their resources. Lives unencumbered by dysfunctional people. You must believe that you can become this kind of person if you want to maintain stability and stay free of energy vampires.

I knew a person who had no real happiness in her life for over twenty-five years. Finally, she left her abuser for good and was hired for counter work at a small store. She was ashamed and angry with the world that this was the only job she could get. Her abuser was able to avoid being charged with crimes despite obvious evidence and the involvement of social services and law enforcement. She was angry with life. The judge was unfair, society was unfair, the courts were unfair, and she hated her life and what it had become. She wanted to make change, but change was not progressing fast enough. She hated the world. She felt that life was horribly cruel and she "deserved" better than this.

Allowing your ego to rule your choices will lead only to despair.

We talked about it and I helped her see some positive possibilities. I shared with her the idea that sometimes life demands things from us. I pointed out that we cannot always dictate what life will bring our way, we can only control our actions when life delivers its demands. I reminded her of the radical acceptance that must sometimes be embraced, not out of free choice but out of necessity. I pointed out that her new job was a beginning, not an end. Someone was trusting and believing in her and offering her a chance to prove herself. They knew nothing of her past. They were not responsible for her past. So why was she dwelling on her past? A past that cannot be changed. A past that can be invalidated by new growth. They were not offering her a punishment, only an open, honest chance to prove herself. They were offering her an opportunity within the present moment and they were indifferent to her past. Her past was not factored into their decision to hire her. I asked her some questions. Why was she using her precious present moment to dwell upon the past? How is it useful to dwell upon people who have nothing to do with this present moment? Why was she allowing the past to rent space in her mind and impact a present moment opportunity? Why allow the past to poison the present moment?

She quickly worked her way to various new positions over time. Using her first job after her abuser as a platform, she applied for other jobs. She mastered new skills and gained higher status jobs and eventually she worked herself into a position of responsibility. She now holds a professional position within a prestigious major metropolitan city. She enjoys fine restaurants and activities that were not possible during her life with the narcissist. She drives a new car, the first one she has ever owned. With performance bonuses she makes six figures a year. More money than she ever made living in poverty with an abusive narcissist. She is off enjoying a grand adventure that has become her new life. She is married to a spouse that loves and supports her dreams, and they have a beautiful life together. Not bad for a severely abused woman who started over with no skills and a low paid job. A woman who had to begin her life again after leaving an abusive narcissist. Her old way of life was invalidated by her new growth. It was not easy, and she worked hard, both personally and professionally. She has come a long way from that newly free survivor upset and sad because her first job had her making minimum wage.

"Simple joys are the most lasting joys."

By realizing that her first job free of the vampire was an opportunity rather than a punishment or a chore, she made gradual progress. Her self-esteem grew the old-fashioned way. It grew as she set goals and accomplished those goals. Her first year was all service industry work.

By year two she was investigating opportunities in other states and cities. By year three she had gained some new skills (Word. Excel, and several kinds of accounting software) and she was working for a temp agency. By year four she was unstoppable and had mastered many new software programs. She went grey rock on her narcissist and eventually she overcame the abuse by growing stronger. She moved on. She stopped living in a past that she could not change, and she instead became thankful for the lessons. She accepted that life demanded something of her. She held herself accountable for her decisions. She lost the victim mentality along the way. She grew the most when she surrendered to the demands of life and practiced radical acceptance. She made the fastest progress when she decided to live life in the present moment rather than living her life according to her demands. When she accepted the valuable lessons born of a painful past that she cannot change, she began to glimpse light again. When she accepted the reality of a cruel past that wounded her and taught her those powerful lessons at the same time, she found true purpose. She finally left the darkness behind. She learned the value of service to others, and by doing so she was able to be of service to herself. She found a success that she never dreamed possible. She out pictured a new life that at one time (in her painful past) she could not envision ever attaining. Her old, long discarded narcissist is powerless over her now. She has fiercely outgrown that dysfunctional vampire. The energy leech has been invalidated by her new sense of self.

Since she began practicing acceptance and seeing her life as one of service she has grown in many ways. She has become a source of inspiration just as she was once inspired. The universe has blessed her efforts and she has been a catalyst for growth to others. Besides being in a wonderful relationship with a supportive partner, she has gained a new respect for herself. Her old way of life has been invalidated by new growth. She does not judge others for their past. Instead, just as kind people once did not judge her, but instead gave her an opportunity, she brings light, never darkness. When she felt worthless, someone saw worth within her and she has passed this gift on to others, quietly and humbly, just as it was given to her.

Lord, grant that I might not so much

Seek to be loved as to love.

- St. Francis of Assisi

She felt hopeless and disconnected from life when she was living with the minion of chaos. She felt lost and ungrounded. She was unable to envision herself in a life of her own making and choosing. She saw herself as a victim and possessed virtually no self-esteem. She eventually built self-esteem the old-fashioned way; she accepted her opportunity as a beginning and not an end. She saw it as a blessing, not a punishment. She set goals and she accomplished them. By embracing acceptance and walking behind that counter that first day it was offered to her, she set herself upon a path to happiness as yet unknown to her.

Free people know that life demands things from us, and we are entitled to nothing except what we earn by our own, honest effort.

Leaving the narcissist can be a tough beginning, *but it is a beginning*. It is not the end. Please realize that your first job, free of the narcissist, is also not an ending. It too is just a beginning. You never know where a positive attitude will lead you because you cannot see the future. Just know with all certainty that your choices within the present moment are shaping your future. A sure and certain future you cannot see until it becomes your present moment down the road. You are traveling with thought guiding you. Travel your road away from the narcissist with a positive attitude, acceptance, a sense of service to others, and wise choices. Your choices will determine your life.

Your past is only an ancient reflection of old choices invalidated by new growth within the present moment. Choose wisely.

Narcopaths are dysfunctional people. They dwell in darkness and call it light. They live, breathe, and create chaos and call it peace. Hating them for their obvious pathology will not sustain you. Resenting the vampire for its present or past role in your life is an exercise in futility. Resentment cannot heal you, thus it is useless. This is also dysfunctional thinking and it cannot serve your higher good. This indulgence in darkness of the soul is not in your rational self-interest. It cannot lead you into light. Remember that resentment and its co-occurring anger are secondary emotions. You are most likely angry at a cluster of resentments due to your past choices. You can own those choices and accept the power within the lessons. You may resent the narcissistic abuse process, this is normal at first. You may be ashamed of your accepted role within the relationship. You may resent the social service system, which can be less than warm and fuzzy at times. Especially so when it comes to recognizing narcissistic abuse victims. The narcissist in your life represents betrayal, abuse, loss, pain, and the result of past choices. The creature also presented powerful lessons. You may not be happy with your past choices. Deep down you may be unhappy with yourself, your decisions, and possibly your life currently. Secretly you worry that you will attract another narcissist or make unwise choices in the future. *It does not have to stay this way. Accept the power of the lessons life has given you. Move forward with the confidence of lessons learned well. Accept the secret gift. Dump the chump.*

No narcissist ever asked for you by name. The vampire appeared, and it was invited into your life due to choices you made. You entered their world by making a choice. They didn't enter your world without your permission. You drew them to you by your choices and your decision to make those choices. They had no choice in meeting you, they were just obeying their instinct driven

behavior as all animals must do. You had the choice to avoid them. You might have side-stepped them entirely by recognizing their dysfunctional behavior. You chose the opposite because of hope, empathy, compassion, and misplaced "love." You were unable to recognize the toxic nightmare coming your way. Like a person blind in a hurricane, you stumbled as best you could. You made your decisions based on your gifts of awareness at the time. It may be your fault they are in your life however you know better now. There is no reason to be harsh on yourself over the past. No predatory animal ever had the option of hanging up an "I'm not hungry" sign. You have a new awareness now. You have learned some harsh and powerful lessons. You have new tools in your tool chest. Use them.

You can choose how you deal with this situation. You can devote yourself to yourself in a healthy way. Working long hours, working two jobs, or an extra part time job, working and going to school, these are actions respected by free society. It has been a tried and true method of success for centuries. It involves setting goals and working to accomplish them. It fills up your self-esteem tank quite nicely. My father did it to get through law school and pay the bills. A good friend did it for a down payment on a house. You can do it also. It is always your choice. It is in your best survival interests to learn the red flags of dysfunctional people and avoid them. It is also in your best interest to cultivate being assertive, not aggressive, being respectful, not afraid, and above all, hard working.

Be the person your employer can rely upon to be on time, to get things done, to come early and stay late.

Consider the virtue of service to others. I do not mean becoming a doormat. Service is a powerful catalyst for change. Service is rewarding in ways much more satisfying than the monetary reward. *Acceptance, service, and surrender* are powerful forces that you can harness to propel your efforts in the workplace to levels you didn't know existed. They are hallmarks of strength, not weakness. *Accept your situation.* You are a survivor putting your life back together. You are beginning again and that is a great thing to do. Becoming employed is a much-needed survival tool in your life. You will have challenges. Your past habits will need examination. Your acceptance of the dysfunctional narcissistic relationship will have to be addressed. You may need to think long and hard about your childhood or family interactions. Future narcissists you have not yet met are in our world. They all have the ability and power to take your freedom again if you allow them to do so. Accept the reality of your current situation. Now is a time for your empowerment. Now is the time for you to grow and learn new skills. Now is the time to allow so much sunlight into your life that future vampires avoid you.

I would like you to consider the meaning of the word "survival." Webster's New World Dictionary, Third College Edition defines survival as "The act, state, or fact of surviving." It goes on to define survival as "Something or someone who survives." Researching a bit further in Webster's we find the word "Survive." The definition of survive I like best is "To continue to live after or in spite of." The example used in Webster's Dictionary is: "To continue to live after, or in spite of, a shipwreck." If you are in a relationship with a narcissist your life is officially a "shipwreck." You are not sailing through life, you are crashing upon the rocks of narcissistic abuse. No ship ever created can sail upon rocks. I call upon you to survive and thrive after the vampire. You have the tools.

Service to others from a place of strength is a truly wonderful thing. When you make one person smile you automatically smile with them. This is powerful because it reflects the best within our human existence. Finding true purpose in service is a beautiful road to travel. It will guide you to developing inner purpose. This road can only lead away from becoming food for a vampire. Finding purpose within service to others is the only true freedom. You cannot see the future, but you can always see the path in front of you as you walk that path. Choosing service is choosing a new life.

Your choices within the present moment become your future. Your choices determine your life.

Surrender is often a misunderstood concept by people overcoming narcissistic abuse. Survivors often do not realize the power within surrender. Post narcissist you are in the process of creating a new life by making different life choices. Surrender in the context of recreation means to let go of an old way of being in the world. You let go of everything that no longer serves your higher good. You release anger, resentment, regret, and fear. You recognize the lessons. You begin to consider your own rational self-interest. This is not done from a place of selfishness. The lessons and their co-occurring insight will arrive from a place open to new beginnings. A place that springs from new found inner strength. You are not "giving up" on life, you are surrendering old ways and choices that cannot serve your present positive situation. Far from being defeated, you are empowered when you let go of old, destructive habits and choices. Release everything invalidated by new growth. Acceptance, service and surrender are your new tools in your survival tool chest. Use them with respect and they will serve you well.

Consider the positive possibilities.

I recommend that you be honest and up front about your lack of job experience with potential employers because self-honesty will serve you well in the long run. Self-honesty is a powerful strength, not a weakness. Self-honesty is the opposite of the ways narcissists portray themselves. I have interviewed too many clients who have lost their jobs due to not being fully honest on an employment application. Simply list the jobs you have actual experience with, also list any courses you completed, and be honest. If you are never up to this first challenge you will limit your job growth and advancement. Also, you will always feel the same stress you felt with the vampire. You will have that "Walking on eggshells" feeling. Gaining a position via exaggeration can quickly become an uncomfortable situation. Being honest with an employer up front stops a whole lot of negativity and drama down the road.

Do not try to fool everyone.

I had a client who felt worthless after he was discarded by his narcissistic wife. He had been raised by a narcissistic mother and his self-esteem was non-existent. He grew up being beaten with belt buckles, electrical cords, coat hangers, and once at the age of seven years old, his mother had hit him in the head with a baseball bat. His alcohol abusing stepfather was an attorney, so his mother was enabled as well as protected from her insane and cruel behavior. The psychological messages he internalized had shaped his psyche to always envision and expect hopelessness. She got away with her abuse and denied it until she passed away. She would never admit her cruelty, nor would she go to counseling other than court ordered anger management that she could not avoid. She took her darkness to her grave. After the Army he married a woman who looked nothing like his mother, however she was a psychological copy of her in almost every way. He didn't know the signs of malignant narcissism and he was conditioned by his mother to accept the unacceptable. Convinced he was unlovable by his mother, he chose a wife who was incapable of love. His 15-year marriage ended after the abnormal drama of living with a narcissist reached its predictable conclusion. He was drained dry of almost all resources having allowed himself to be used for years. He was discarded, and his vampire monkey branched to another victim. Finally, after almost destroying his life with drugs he had a series of epiphanies. He had worked hard for those insights. When drugs didn't work, he sought counseling and read extensively, looking for answers. After his drug charges he was unable to find work other than food service work. He started over and worked hard. He gained self-esteem the old-fashioned way. He set goals and he accomplished them. Today he is a counselor and he helps people find their own light when they can only envision darkness. He began his journey to healthy service from a position of uncertainty behind a fast food counter. His turning point came when a priest stated to him "If your ex was the light of your life, you lived in total darkness." The more he let go of the past, the more he understood the powerful lessons. The more lessons he learned, the more he was able to grow stronger by making better decisions.

Your choices within the present moment become your future.

Everything is earned in this world. Your money, opportunities, respect, and your credibility with other people. Survivors learn to not accept the ways of the vampire in their lives ever again. They will not allow the narcissists past abuse to influence their present moment decisions. Often survivors feel that they were stunted and held back by the narcissist. They feel that they should be farther along in life. They probably would be farther along if they had never met the narcissist. This is even more accurate in the case of being raised by narcissists or having abusive siblings. Regret will not accelerate personal growth. Working on goals will guarantee personal growth. Never lie on an application. It may take a little longer to get hired but in the long run it is a lot better for you and your life goals. It is far more positive to get a truthful chance at a job and show your new employer what you can do. They will know what you are truly capable of accomplishing. *Earning real respect is far better than stealing an opportunity with deceit. Growing stronger post narcissist is a challenge never a problem. Challenges can be met and dealt with.*

A survival job is often a necessity as you train for a new career. You can choose to work a survival job and go to training for a better career. Many people have followed this path and are better off for doing so. You can build a resume while you pursue training in a field of your own choosing. If you must struggle for a while in a survival job just remember that you are a work in progress. You are not finished just yet. You are becoming who you want to be. You are busy beginning a new life and letting go of an old way of being in the world.

It is not the end it is a new beginning, a new journey. Start this journey honestly.

Take the time you need for training in a career. Working and training is a time for you to learn new skills, meet new people, and learn new ways of thinking about things. You will network and learn a new way of being in the world. You will gain confidence about life and your place in life. You are not worthless, you are a human being and there is a purpose for you to find and fulfill in life. Searching for that purpose is a rewarding path to lifelong freedom and happiness. You are not condemned to low paying jobs for the rest of your life. No matter your age or your current position, you can still make goals and have higher purpose aspirations. It is up to you alone to identify, choose and pursue those goals. The vampire's opinion does not matter anymore. Your opinion matters now.

We are entitled to nothing except what we earn.

There exist six cold, hard facts about survivors of narcissistic abuse that I will share with you now.

1. You cannot heal the narcissist so do not try to do the impossible.

2. The narcissist will never love you and has never loved you.

3. Survivors will never be understood completely by most people who learn of their past.

4. Society will always judge a survivor harsher. Don't believe me? Look at how your narcopath was able to manipulate counselors, police, judges, attorneys, friends and even your family. Observe how the victims

of narcissistic abuse are often blamed for the twisted behavior of the narcissist. Observe how the victims are blamed for being involved with the narcopath.

5.   You must work smarter and harder than others to obtain what you need.

6.   You must change from within using acceptance, forgiveness, and surrender.

When you meet former friends, family members, and others who judge you by your past life with the narcissist, just know that they are living in the past. Refuse to argue with them. Don't try to "convince" them of anything. It is a waste of time. They are speaking from their ego and the ego just wants to make everyone wrong and itself right. They are trying to bring up your past to make you "wrong" in the present. You are not your past. When you become defensive or argue with them you are just playing ego games. You are doubting yourself and your present moment choices. You are giving away your personal power by accepting their negativity and you are living in the past right alongside them. You are losing time in the present moment. Your energy is focused upon defending your own ego rather than experiencing your new growth or following your new path. You are squandering your energy on the past. Far from being defeated, you are empowered when you surrender. When you let go of old, destructive habits and choices invalidated by the need for new growth, you free yourself. Acceptance, service and surrender are your new tools in your survival tool chest. Use them well and they will serve you well.

Since first impressions are forever, show up to the job interview prepared and on time. Bring extra copies of transcripts, letters of recommendation, your resume, and any job-related certificates you have earned. Allow the interviewer to control the flow and pace of the interview. This may be difficult for you after years of dealing with a narcissist but do it anyway. Do not exaggerate, brag, and never volunteer information about your past that is not specifically asked for by the interviewer. Do not speak ill of former employers, co-workers, or your narcissist, and maintain professional boundaries. Do not smoke and don't ask for a smoke break. Stay off your cell phone.

You have only the present moment, moment to moment, and your choices within each moment will become your future.

Dress modestly and neatly. Do not show up to a job interview wearing formal wear. Don't show up too casual either. *Unless you hate work of course.* Try to research the company online so you come to the interview prepared with some knowledge about the company's mission statement and goals, as well as their products and services. If the interviewer asks you what you know about the company, you will be able to converse with some confidence on the topic. Also try to visit the company site in advance to get an idea about the dress code. If you don't have a computer, ask a friend for help or go to the public library and sign onto a computer there. Do not bring friends and do not have anyone wait in the car for you during the interview process. Make sure your cell phone is turned off.

When you meet new people, you will have only that present moment in time to present yourself. Your choices in language, speech, body language, tone of voice, and facial expressions, will convey an image. That image will be interpreted as "you" by the new people meeting you for the first time. Choose wisely when you present yourself (YOUR-SELF) to the world. You have only the present moment, use that precious moment in time extremely well.

Remember to be honest but it is OK to minimize past challenges whenever possible. You cannot expect people to understand your past challenges with a narcissist or your old, outdated, vampire food lifestyle. Instead of saying you were in an abusive relationship, you might try saying that you are seeking professional growth. Don't make things worse than they really are.

If they ask about gaps in your past employment record let the interviewer know that you are desiring growth and new opportunities. Let them know about current things in your life, training, online classes, hobbies, and healthy pastimes you enjoy in the present. Always bring the conversation back into the present moment whenever possible. Make sure your handshake is warm, firm, and dry. Ask for the interviewer's business card after the job interview. Write them a thank you card and mail it that evening so they remember you. Even if you are not hired now, they may hire you later because they remember you in a positive light.

You have only the present moment, use that precious moment in time extremely well.

I have one more tip about interviews. Bring along a fact sheet to every interview. Have a few copies ready to hand out to the interviewer if needed. A fact sheet is not a resume. A fact sheet has your personal information and references on it. A resume never has references included. A fact sheet has your driver's license number, military information, dates and times of employment, skill and education information and most importantly, current references. You can refer to your fact sheet during the interview process. If references are requested immediately you have them available. A fact sheet also demonstrates how well you have prepared for the interview to the potential employer. *Employers tend to notice and like well-prepared people*.

Do not allow your past to define your present.

Remember that your goal is not just to survive but to eventually thrive. Living well is fun. Work and school are goal-oriented situations for everyone, not just survivors. I am still taking work related courses in counseling and case management after over 20 years in the field. Learning never stops in today's modern workforce. People are always updating skills and learning is considered a lifelong process. You can survive anything with enough hope and desire. You survived life with a narcissist because you had an innate, powerful desire for something better. You associated hope for a better beginning with that powerful realization that life with a narcissist was unacceptable. I recommend that you fill your days with work, training or both. Your continued freedom from narcissistic abuse depends upon it and your future quality of life surely does.

Earning real respect is far better than stealing an opportunity with deceit. Having escaped a narcissistic relationship is a challenge never a problem. Challenges can be met and dealt with. Far from being defeated, you are empowered when you let go of old, destructive habits and choices invalidated by new growth. Acceptance, service and surrender are your new tools in your survival tool chest. Use them well and they will serve you well.

JOB HUNTING IS A JOB.

Make your job hunt a forty hour per week, full time job. Most survivors are so beat down that they put in a few local applications, visit a state employment development office and then lay back to see what happens. Don't be that person because work is a survival tactic. Blanket your city with hundreds of applications. Society tends to respect people who try hard to do the right thing. Most state employment development departments have job centers where you can get help with cover letters and resumes. You will also have access to local job boards and online access to state wide job opportunities as well as training.

Most of these state-run job centers have an employment specialist on site to assist you in a job search.

Temp agencies are also a good resource. Many temp agencies place people in a variety of positions. Employers like temp agencies because they have a chance to see how you work out without a lengthy interview and hiring process. Many temp agency jobs can lead to permanent placement with an employer. The employer saves money and time because they trust the temp agency to screen you. You benefit because you will get a chance to prove yourself with a company that may not have considered you during a standard hiring and interview process. I watched this happen with a person I worked with. She built up such a good reputation with her work ethic that she was offered a job with a fortune 500 company and is now on her way to a six-figure income.

SIGN HUNTING.

"Sign Hunting" is a technique used successfully by many people new or returning to the workforce. Eighty percent of all jobs are not advertised because many businesses hang help wanted signs or use temp agencies. Sign hunting can help you get an interview right on the spot just for inquiring about the job. The benefit to you is that you can often be seen by the person doing the hiring. Sign hunting simply means that you canvass your community and local industrial parks for help wanted signs, fill out applications, and hopefully meet people along the way.

Make sure to bring your fact sheet with you and have a lot of copies ready. Resumes tend to be screening tools. Most survivors just beginning to start their lives over have a hard time getting a chance when they have no current jobs to put on a resume. Sign hunting can get you started in the employment world. Remember, you are looking for a beginning, not an "end."

NETWORKING.

Do not hesitate to use support group contacts for job opportunities. Let people know at group meetings that you have employment challenges. You must learn to ask for help when you need it. If you attend a place of worship let the pastor, rabbi, priest, or Imam know that you are hunting for a job. Let them know about the challenges you face as a survivor. Also, don't forget about your local public library and college job boards. Both places have resources you can use to find work. Library's also have the latest local paper and computers for you to use for online applications.

Do not forget local union halls when considering opportunities for work. A survivor in his early fifties started out as a laborer in the iron workers union and within two years he was a union welder. *Good things happen when you refuse to give up and decide to make things happen.*

Do not allow your past to define your present moment choices.

YOUR RESUME.

A resume is a screening tool and as I pointed out earlier it can be a blessing or a curse for some people. If you have been trapped in a narcissistic nightmare for many years and have gained few vocational or educational skills while in living hell, a resume will most likely screen you out of a job. I recommend that you use sign hunting, networking, temp agencies and the local state job center for your employment challenges. Remember that most of the time you create your own luck. If you have some vocational training and a past employment history, then I recommend that you use the local job center for a resume workshop. These classes are ongoing, and you will get help with cover letters, free copies, and most importantly, the current resume and cover letter formats that employers are seeking. Employers regularly throw away resumes that are in an outdated style or the wrong kind of paper. The cover letter format seems to change with resumes every few years. Your best strategy is to use the formats that the local employment development department recommends in your state.

TOOLS.

The following items will make your future work and personal life much easier. These are not just tools for people restarting their lives, they are tools for life. Almost everyone in the free world uses these tools regularly.

1. A watch. It does not have to be a Rolex or a Swiss Watch, it just needs to be accurate.

2. A small notebook for addresses and phone numbers as a backup to your cell phone.

3. A pen. For your notebook and life in general.

4. A calendar. One for your home and one for work. Make sure it has room for you to write all over it.

5. A cell phone. You need one for communication as pay phones are almost non-existent. There are apps available for every one of the afore mentioned tools just for your cell phone but always have a backup. Always have a car charger and a regular charger for your phone.

6. Laptop or notebook computer. If you don't have one now get one. Learn to use them well. The world is fast, and you will have to keep up. Classes are offered in some stores and most computers come with built in tutorials, so you can literally "plug and go."

Once you develop the smart habit of using your notebook and calendars your life will be more organized and simpler to manage. Your calendar is the place for all work and social obligations to be displayed. Birthdays, holidays, meetings, your work schedule, all these belong on your calendar. Always remember to backup all numbers in your electronic devices and to keep a copy in your paper notebook.

Stay focused on the present moment, not the past.

Make sure you use that watch and be punctual. People will judge you in the free world by how you use and manage time. Being responsible with time and accomplishing tasks will benefit you in many ways. You will accomplish more, feel better, and gain more control of your life. You will also gain self-esteem, and grow in satisfaction with yourself, your goals, and your life overall.

MEETINGS WITH POSSIBLE EMPLOYERS.

Record in your paper and electronic notebooks as well as your calendar all meetings with future employers. Every date and time, what you discussed, your obligations met and unmet. If your employer/interviewer gave you instructions, record the dates and times you carried out those instructions. Record the dates and times of all job required urine tests and the outcomes. Record your compliance with all registration or testing requirements that you have been asked to comply with.

It is not the end it is a new beginning, a new journey. Start this journey honestly.

Do not use the top of your refrigerator or TV as a filing cabinet. If you don't have a filing cabinet buy one and use it. Buy some file folders and a cardboard box if that is all you can afford at first. Begin to keep records now. You are learning to live as a free person post narcissist and this takes some effort and planning on your part. Sitting on the couch eating chips will not do it for you. Other people will not do it for you. Living vampire free and drama free is a journey. It will require some time, accountability, and energy on your part. You will not have time for old, outdated, negative thinking errors or victim thinking. Your old way of life will become invalidated by the new growth inherent within meeting the challenges of vampire free life.

Far from being defeated, you are empowered when you let go of old, destructive habits and choices invalidated by the need for new growth. Acceptance, service and surrender are your new tools in your survival tool chest. Use them well and they will serve you well. Your choices within the present moment become your future.

Chapter eight Exercises.

1.   Lookup three temporary employment agencies in your area. Write them each a letter and request information about their services. Be sure to enclose a stamped, addressed envelope for them to respond to you with. If they like to respond electronically (Most do) then e-mail each of them and ask about their services. Follow up with a phone call and make an appointment.

2. Look up the address and website for your local employment development department. Explore their website in depth. Call them and ask about their services for job seekers. Make sure to request information on any seminars and specific services that can be of help to you. Make an appointment to learn about their services and opportunities and show up 15 minutes early.

Look up the following words and write out the definitions.

Image.

Work.

Need.

Want.

Vampire free people know that life demands things from us, and we are entitled to nothing except what we earn. Your past is only an ancient reflection of old choices invalidated by new growth. Your future is being created by your new choices within the present moment. Choose wisely.

Chapter Eight

Personal Development Questions.

1.   Describe your work ethic in three paragraphs.

2.   Describe your ideal career.

Good things happen when you refuse to give up and decide to make things happen.

Chapter Eight Affirmations: I am created from universal abundance.

I am universal abundance.

I effortlessly attract opportunities to serve others in all I do.

I am grateful for all lessons learned.

Chapter Nine

Take back your power

Are you happy living with an abuser? Only you can make yourself happy. You may be happy when other people are in your life, but they cannot make you happy. True inner happiness comes from living an inspired life. What inspires you? Are you following that inspiration? I ask these questions because I want you to begin to consider these questions. There is one defining characteristic common to all the billions of humans living upon spaceship earth. We all seek happiness in one form or another. Your past lifestyle with the narcissist was (at its core,) concerned with seeking happiness. You were willing to sacrifice your happiness to try and "succeed" in that dysfunctional relationship.

Happiness is a universal need, yet the true nature of happiness eludes most people everywhere. Not just people trapped within narcissistic relationships. The true nature of happiness is always singular. The fact that you are a unique individual will guarantee that your personal definition of happiness will be different than other people's definitions. It is your job to find happiness for yourself. No one else can do that for you. No matter how wonderful or horrible another human being treats you, you have the answer to internal happiness. No matter how cruel or comfortable your external world is at this time, your own happiness can only be found within yourself.

KEEP AND MAINTAIN A JOURNAL

Write in your journal every day. It must be in a secure location. I cannot emphasize this enough. If you are in a vampire infected relationship right now, then I recommend you wait until post- vampire. The only exception is based upon how secure you can keep the journal. Unless you can keep it secure, secret, and vampire free do not chance the creature reading it. The narcopath will use and abuse anything it can pre and post discard. The abuser will try to harm you psychologically, emotionally, and possibly physically. Private journals are a creeps favorite tool for exploitation against their target.

When you can journal safely please do so. A journal can help you heal and give you great perspective. Your personal journal can lead to great personal insights. Just make sure the vampire never sees it, finds it, or reads it. If you miss a day due to work, life, or family it is ok. Write again tomorrow. Writing in a journal helps you to get to know yourself better. When I use the term "yourself" I mean your true, authentic self. Not the self you present while in a dysfunctional relationship. Your real self. To make and maintain positive change and gain your own internal happiness you must meet four challenges. A journal will help you do this.

1. You must become you own best and closest friend.

2. You must make peace with your past as best you can.

3. You must know, understand, and accept your life right up to this point.

4. You must practice being in the moment because the present moment is all you have.

The past is dead; you are not your past. The future has not yet happened. You have only the present moment, moment to moment, and your choices within each moment will become your future. Seeing this process can begin growth in a new direction.

Have you ever talked yourself out of leaving the vampire? Have you ever talked yourself out of a raise? Have you ever cut classes or not studied because you just "knew" you wouldn't pass the test anyway? Have you ever met an attractive person you wanted to ask out and then lost your nerve? Have there been jobs you were interested in, yet you never applied for those jobs because of the fear of being rejected? Have you failed to speak up for yourself due to frustration or the rationalization that nobody understands you anyway?

How do you transform yourself, that person in the mirror, into your closest friend? You acknowledge yourself, accept your struggle, and surrender your old ways that no longer serve your best interests. You discard anything and anyone that opposes your healing. You must begin to act in your own rational self-interest. You must allow some "healthy selfishness" into your life if you hope to foster new growth. By doing these things you achieve psychological freedom from your own (old) past personal history. It is important to "own" your "old" past because it is then that you accept the lessons learned. Within acceptance comes the movement to newness. Your new personal history is being written right now, even as you read this book. *Every present moment, moment to moment, travels towards the future. Your choices and thoughts within those countless present moments are precious. They are creating your future and writing your history simultaneously.* You do not have to allow the ghosts of past choices to haunt you forever. New choices will eventually run them off for good.

When you journal, examine your past choices, look at and explore options you did not know you had at the time. Journal what you would do differently if you could do it all over. Journal about how you have changed in your outlook. Journal about challenges within your present moment. Journal your new life history a sentence at a time, a paragraph at a time. Your journal will become a map of your personal growth and progress. Your journal will become a way to look back at where you have been with acceptance and surrender. It is a powerful tool for consciousness expansion. A way to move forward with courage, hope, insight, and gratitude within the present moment. A journal will help you recognize the hard-earned lessons of your journey. A journal is empowering.

The past is dead, you are not your past. The future has not yet happened. You have only the present moment, moment to moment, and your choices within each moment will become your future. Seeing this process can begin growth in a new direction. Consider the positive possibilities. You had freedom from choice with the abuser, you have freedom of choice now. What will you do?

Seek out new experiences when you are finally post-narcissist. Journal these new experiences. Try new foods, listen to different music, meet new people, learn a new sport, and join new clubs. Mabey you would like to try a computer club or an archery club. Find out. You are free to learn a martial art, a new language, or a musical instrument. Join a gym and then *Journal it all.* The more you explore and practice making new choices the better off your life will become in the long run. The more chances you self-create for finding a passion, a driving force in your life that becomes your new purpose. Once you begin living with purpose you will be immersed in happiness. You will be thriving not just surviving. Your old, self-destructive way of life will be a distant memory. Your new, purpose driven life will consume you and you will have found fulfillment.

Consider what "Purpose" means to you. The narcissist has an instinct driven purpose. It needs to feed on other peoples' attention, resources, energy, and it needs to manipulate its environment accordingly. Drama and discord are the hallmarks of the narcissist. Resenting the narcissist for its' vampire-like nature is an exercise in futility. It just engages your brain and starts the chemical cascade that begins your descent back into the past and into regret. Resentment can be invalidated by new growth. Choose to grow away from your old life with the vampire. The vampire feeds upon energy. It does not care if the energy is positive or negative. It craves energy, your energy. Don't let the vampire rent space in your brain and don't feed its toxic ghost when you have moved on.

Resentment only stifles your growth from expanding in new, positive directions. It diverts you from finding your own, authentic purpose. Unlike the instinctive, pathological driven purpose of the vampire, a healthy human being must find their purpose. To accomplish this, humans must face their fears. Unlike the narcissist, humans must not be driven by instinct, they must find a way to manage their instincts. You are the only person who can find your own unique purpose.

Remember: Healthy people understand that life demands things from us, and we are entitled to nothing except what we earn and what we learn. Your past is only an ancient reflection of old choices invalidated by new growth and new choices within the present moment. Choose wisely. The past is dead, you are not your past. The past lives on only within your mind with your full permission. The future has not yet happened. You have not yet brought it into being. You have only the present moment, moment to moment, and your choices within each moment will influence and eventually become your future. Seeing this process can begin growth in a new direction. Consider the positive possibilities. You chose freedom from choice within the narcissist-controlled relationship. You have total freedom of choice now. What will you do with your freedom to choose?

Far from being defeated, you are empowered when you surrender and let go of old, destructive relationships, habits, and choices invalidated by the need for new growth. Acceptance of your past, rational self-interest, and surrender to your highest good are your new tools in your survival tool chest. Use them well and they will serve you well. Your choices within the present moment become your future. A survivor does not expect others to make survival choices for them.

Allowing your ego to rule your choices leads only to despair. Don't adopt the narcissist's way of being in the world. Everyone else will be wrong and you will always be right. You will win every battle and lose the ultimate war for your freedom. Even when you are free of the vampire, you will be psychologically trapped. You will think like a victim and act like a victim. You will eventually return to the place where vampires feed and victims live out their lives. All of it will reflect your choices.

If you really knew how to have a healthy relationship, what were you doing allowing a vampire to feed upon you? You are not your anger. You are not your resentment. Your past is only an ancient reflection of old choices invalidated by new growth within the present moment. You are not your past. You own this present moment. You are who you choose to become. Your response is all yours, always. You cannot control what others do and say but you have total control over what you do and say. Consider the positive possibilities.

When you meet people, who judge you by your past just know that they are living in the past. Refuse to argue with them. Don't try to "convince" them of anything. It is a waste of time. They are using narcissistic tactics. They are speaking from their ego and the ego just wants to make everyone wrong and itself right, always. The toxic ego needs constant defending. They are trying to bring up your past to make you "wrong" within the present moment. You are not your past. When you become defensive or argue with them you are just playing ego games. You are doubting yourself and your present moment choices. You are giving away your personal power by accepting their negativity. You are living in the past right alongside them. You are losing time in the present moment and your energy is focused on defending your own ego rather than your new growth, your new path. You are squandering your energy upon the past. Return to the present moment always. Their judgment of your past is not your present. Leave judgement behind along with the abusive vampire.

Chapter Eight Affirmations:

I am a being becoming, no longer bound by my past.

I enjoy creating my perfect future within my present moment.

I have reclaimed my personal power.

Remember the rules of rational self-care:

I told you in the beginning of this book that I would remind you of them. I hope you love them.

It is not in your rational self-interest to stay in any relationship that is ruled by habitual deceit, dishonesty, cruelty, and violence.

You can leave any situation where you feel unloved. This includes leaving toxic family members as well as romantic partners or negative "friends." People incapable of empathy or compassion cannot "love" anyone. They cannot be authentic "friends "with anyone. You cannot "fix" them. Staying around abusive idiots because they are "family" has destroyed countless lives. Don't fall for the myth of "They are family." You had no choice in the family you were born into. You do have the choice to reject mistreatment, abuse, and insulting behavior.

You can choose to be "Better off without them." This is perfectly OK.

You can leave any relationship that is destroying your capacity for growth, self-acceptance, and self-love. This also includes leaving or avoiding harmful family members. Insults and negative judgements both obvious and veiled, are completely unacceptable.

You can reject shaming language directed at you by anyone. You owe no one an explanation as to why you choose to avoid them. Shaming language is just cruelty in a weak disguise. Shaming language is sadistic language. Shaming language is always an attempt to control you.

You can decide to go "No contact" with anyone who is abusive, disrespectful, rude, insulting, crass, vulgar, or derogatory towards you. You do not have to explain your decision to anyone.

You can leave anyone at any time who tries to keep you enmeshed within the darkness of pain, guilt, regret, and insult. The past cannot be changed. Actions and beliefs in the present moment direct your future. You are under no obligation to allow abusive idiots to influence your present moment. No one has the right to constantly use your past against you. Using your past as a weapon to hurt, control, or shame you is automatic grounds for rejection. Relational violence does not have to be physical violence to cause lasting damage.

You do not have to stay trapped in any location, city, or town. Don't sacrifice your inspiration for a location. It may take work and careful planning, but you can leave.

You, and only you are the final authority on what is important to you.

You are allowed to "begin again." This means unlimited fresh starts and do-overs. No exceptions to this rule.

You define your life path, no one else does this for you. Don't allow them to even attempt it.

You and only you decide your personal reality. This includes your gender, attraction, beliefs, spirituality, and what makes you happy. Attraction is not a "choice." Your attraction is authentic because it is something unique to you. Attraction, gender, beliefs, and spirituality are uniquely individual traits. No one else's opinion matters regarding your personal choices. They belong to you alone.

You are allowed to leave when you are hurt emotionally, physically, or psychologically. You need only your permission to do so.

You and only you decide what hurts you emotionally, physically, or psychologically.

You can put your healing first, at anytime and anywhere.

You can reject anyone who wants to keep you enmeshed within an abusive dynamic. (This especially includes harmful, dangerous, cruel, and abusive family members.)

You can allow kind, understanding, and authentic people into your life.

You can allow healthy love into your life.

You and only you select your support team.

You can forgive yourself for all current and past errors involving judgement, misdeeds, imperfections, or wrongdoings.

You can release the past whenever you decide to do so.

You can change directions at any time you choose to do so. Making the decision to no longer stay trapped with toxic people in negative spaces is not "Being weak," "giving up," or "quitting." It is having the strength to seek a healthier way of being in the world. It is seeking to empower yourself and love yourself. It is recognizing the drive and need for a new life when an old way of life is finally invalidated by new growth.

You are allowed to decide for yourself when to move on and when to stay hopeful. You are the best person suited for that decision.

You can admit that leaving the abuser is part of your rational self-care.

You can ignore other people's negative expectations, negative messages, as well as your own negative self-talk.

Chapter Ten

Resources

Alcoholics Anonymous. <u>*www.aa.org*</u> *AA World Services, PO Box 459 Grand Central Station, New York, N.Y. 10163*

Narcotics Anonymous. <u>*www.na.org*</u> *NA World Services, PO Box 9999 Van Nuys, CA 91409 Phone 1-818-773-9999*

AL Anon and AlATeen national headquarters: https:// www.alanon-maryland.org/baltimore-contacts/world-service-office-wso/

The Salvation Army. <u>*www.salvationarmy.org*</u> *For prison ministries and prisoner resources:* <u>*http://www. salvationarmyusa.org/usa/prison-ministries*</u>*, Salvation Army National Headquarters, 615 Slaters Lane PO Box 269, Alexandria VA 22313*

Catholic Charities, 2050Ballenger Ave. Suite 400 Alexandria, VA 22314 Phone (703)-549-1390 <u>*www. catholiccharities.org*</u>

Khan Academy offers free, online courses to the people of earth. You can find courses on a wide variety of subjects and it is all free. Khan academy is a non-profit organization and they do accept donations.

https://www.khanacademy.org/

Sometimes you need some help in understanding your actual situation. The website below offers you the ability to see the possible threats you face in a dysfunctional relationship. This site is only for you, do not allow the narcissist to know you have used it as a resource. Keep the results secret.

https://www.mosaicmethod.com/

"Just know with all certainty that your choices within the present moment are shaping your future, a future you cannot see until it becomes your present moment down the road you are traveling. Travel your road with a positive attitude, acceptance, a healthy sense of service to others coupled with rational self-interest, and wise choices. Your choices will determine your life."

Some useful and interesting terms often used in the narcopathic abuse recovery community:

Narc: A short abbreviation for Narcissist.

Flying Monkeys: A term derived from the minions used by the wicked witch in the film "The Wizard of OZ." A flying monkey is a person who is used, manipulated, or fooled into helping the narcissist achieve and maintain his control, discard, manipulation, or torture over the narcissist's victim.

Triangulation: A manipulation technique used by the narcissist to control and direct the flow of information between people. The narcissist has a pathological need to have all communication center upon him and his goals. Triangulation is a means to make sure that all communication is interpreted favorably towards the narcissist and supports his goals.

Narcopath: This term was first used on the internet to describe someone who has the traits/patterns of both a severe sociopath and a narcissist. I see narcissism as just part of the spectrum of anti-social personality disorders. Narcopath is useful in identifying a dangerous, dysfunctional, abusive individual with both narcissist and anti-social patterns. I believe that narcissism is on the spectrum of sociopath/psychopath.

Hoovering; this usually is a pattern observed after no contact has been in place for a while. The narcissist tries to reconnect with his victim after losing his supply.

Love Bombing: Literally being bombed with false affection. Narcissists like to move in on their targets with lighting speed. Terms like "You get me" and "soul mate" will be used. If it seems too good to be true, it probably is too good to be true.

No Contact: The narcissist and anyone still in contact with the narcissist is totally ignored. The abuser and associates are not interacted with on even a superficial level. Flying monkeys are especially ignored. The narcissist uses emotional manipulation to "capture" its prey. Faking emotions and mimicking empathy or compassion is just a survival tool to a narcissist. It cannot "get better." Recovery requires no contact or limited contact (in the case of shared children) because a narcissist cannot communicate in a healthy way with a healthy human being.

Gaslighting: The term comes from an old movie whereby a husband tricks his wife into thinking she is insane. With narcissists it usually comes in the form of a "joke" that was really a veiled insult. The narcissist will then insist that it was not an insult, and insist you are defective in that you lack a sense of humor. You are labeled "crazy" for noticing anything dysfunctional within the relationship.

Trauma bonded: This often happens when a person was abused and manipulated intermittently within a high stress environment. For example: a child who is raised in a dangerous, unhealthy home environment might grow up to be vulnerable to being trapped in abusive relationships. In adults' trauma bonding can involve the abuser using fear, violence, excitement, anticipation, sexual interaction and separation to control and manipulate their victim. Toxic trauma bonding can become the "Go-to relationship" for an abuse victim. Abusive relationships can become a repetitive reality. The partners may change but the dysfunctional dynamic will stay the same. It was Patrick Carnes that developed the term "Trauma Bonding." Many victims of domestic violence and sexual abuse are especially vulnerable to trauma bonding.